IN THE NAME
OF THE FAMILY

Also by Judith Stacey

Brave New Families: Stories of Domestic Upheaval
in Late Twentieth-Century America
Patriarchy and Socialist Revolution in China

IN THE NAME
OF THE FAMILY

Rethinking Family Values
in the Postmodern Age

· · · · · · · · · ·

Judith Stacey

Beacon Press
Boston

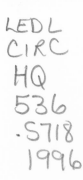
Beacon Press
25 Beacon Street
Boston, Massachusetts 02108-2892

Beacon Press books
are published under the auspices of
the Unitarian Universalist Association of Congregations.

02 01 00 99 98 97   8 7 6 5 4 3 2

Text design by Nancy A. Crompton

Library of Congress Cataloging in Publication Data can be found on page 196.

An earlier version of chapter one, "Backward toward the Postmodern Family," first
appeared in America at Century's End, Alan Wolfe, ed. Berkeley and Los Angeles:
University of California Press, 1991. Chapter two, "The Family Is Dead; Long Live
Our Families" revises an essay commissioned and published by Sociology Database,
Craig Calhoun and George Ritzer, eds. McGraw Hill, 1994. An early version of
Chapter three, "The Neo-Family-Values Campaign," first appeared in Social Text
n. 40 (Fall 1994). Chapter four, "Virtual Social Science and the Politics of Family
Values" is a revised version of a chapter originally prepared for inclusion in Critical
Anthropology in Fin-De-Siècle America: New Locations, Non-Standard Fieldwork.
George Marcus, ed. Santa Fe: School of American Research, forthcoming. Chapter
five, "Gay and Lesbian Families Are Here; All Our Families Are Queer; Let's Get
Used to It!" is a version of a chapter commissioned for publication in The Evolving
American Family. Steven Sugarman, Mary Ann Mason, and Arlene Skolnick, eds.
New York: Oxford University Press, forthcoming.

To Jake
and inclusive social values

Contents

. . . .

Acknowledgments

. . . .

"It takes a village to raise a book," as my dear friends and colleagues, Fred Block and Carole Joffe like to quip. Living in the age of electronic media, I called upon a far-flung global village to help me parent this one. To begin with, Marya Van't Hul, my gifted, gracious editor at Beacon Press, truly served as this book's genitor. It was the gleam in her editorial eye that planted the seed that generated this project. Since its conception, Marya has nurtured, counseled, and cheered its growth with that magical blend of wisdom, enthusiasm and responsibility with which all "children" might flourish, but far too few are blessed.

Numerous other village elders and youngsters, near and far, shared with me their tribal wisdom, skills, resources, labor and support. Many of the ideas developed in this book first sprouted, were honed and tested in the stimulating, high-spirited, high caloric gatherings of my Berkeley family politics discussion group, in the thoughtful company of Arlene Skolnick, Jane Mauldon, Joan Hollinger, Joanna Weinberg, Carole Joffe and Diane Ehrensaft. Each shares much of the credit, but none of the responsibility for the many traces of our collective thinking this book displays. Likewise, this textual progeny derived enormous educational benefit from the lively, challenging, sometimes beneficially discordant sessions of the Berkeley Family Research and Public Policy Forum, which has met nearly

x

Acknowledgments

monthly during the past three years under the expert and hospitable leadership of Steve Sugarman and Mary Ann Mason.

Treasured colleagues, friends, relatives and unrelated sages offered invaluable responses to earlier drafts of all or most of the manuscript. For such consistently reliable and nurturant, intellectual and editorial co-parenting, I gratefully thank Barrie Thorne, Carole Joffe, Judith Newton, Herb Schreier, John Gillis, Jeff Escoffier, Arlene Skolnick, Gail Saliterman, Debby Rosenfelt and Pierre Donatien. Among the many others who have generously responded to individual chapters or intellectual puzzles at one time or another, I warmly thank Hanne Haavind, Sherry Ortner, George Marcus, Nicole Berner, Deirdre English, Mary Ryan, Doug Foster, Bill Skinner, and Judy Walkowitz. I have presented earlier versions of most of these chapters at seminars, conferences and public lectures in the U.S., Europe and Israel, where hosts, respondents, students and panelists helped me to rethink their many deficiencies. I particularly wish to thank my hosts and participants in: the 1994 seminar on Power/Knowledge in Fin-de-Siècle U.S.A. convened by George Marcus at the School of American Research; the 1994 International Leadership seminar on Women, Family and Society convened by Fannette Modek at the Golda Meir Center, Haifa, Israel; the 1994 conference on New Horizons or Backlash convened by Ursulla Mueller, Marlene Stein-Hilbers and Christof Armbruster at Bielefeld University in Germany; the plenary session of the 1995 Congress of Swiss Social Sciences organized by Claudia Honnegger; my 1995 Visiting Scholar lectures at the Institute for Advanced Studies in Vienna organized by Christine Goldberg; and public lectures I have delivered at Johns Hopkins University, Wesleyan University, University of Missouri, Lewis & Clark College, University of Oregon, University of California, Berkeley and University of Southern California.

Absolutely indispensable to the book's gestation and timely delivery were the often heroic bibliographic and intellectual labors of Maureen Sullivan, my graduate research assistant whose own "pregnant" doctoral research on lesbian co-parent families did much to inspire and inform chapter five. Likewise, my delightful undergraduate student assistants, Renee Perry and Jenafir House, contributed the sort of enthusiastic, tireless and tedious labors on frantic, last minute bibliographic chores that one would hate to have to impose on one's closest kin. In the midst of the current anti-welfare climate, it seems urgent to underscore that such invaluable "family assistance" depended upon the dole of faculty research grants awarded by the University of California, Davis and by an infusion of a timely additional "block grant" generously bestowed by Alan Olmstead, Director of the Institute of Governmental Affairs at UCD. Expert and compassionate copy editor, Kathy Glidden, lent the manuscript the neighborly helping hand with spring housecleaning chores that it sorely needed.

Finally, one of the troubling paradoxes for those of us who raise books about families is that doing so forces us to divert care and attention from our own. Magnanimously placing their own family values above their self-interests once more, Herb and Jake, my next-of-kin, avidly encouraged me to break the promise they had exacted after they had suffered through the growth pains of my previous books—"never again!" Both cut me more than the usual slack on my share of domestic time and labor while they cheered me on and cheered me up. In exchange, the only promise they solicited from me this time was to forgo my mawkish impulse to give public thanks as well to our household's newest members—Chase and Manhattan, the two, mischievous foundling cats I adopted just in time to help me shred the epidemic of stubborn, paper weeds that seem to sprout in every book grower's wordy garden. Fortunately, irony ranks high among our family values.

Introduction

. . . .

As governor, I can tell you that about 80 percent of the problems that hit my desk you can trace back to the breakdown of the family structure in our society, and I think anyone who doesn't want to admit that is kidding themselves.

—*Illinois Governor Jim Edgar, November 1995*

We've got to end welfare politics that discourage marriage and reward irresponsible behavior. . . . There's a popular saying that "it takes an entire village to raise a child." The fact is, the village can help, but a child's future will really be determined by just two villagers—mom and dad.

—*California Governor Pete Wilson, State of
the State Address, January 1996*

The feminist agenda is not about equal rights for women. It is a socialist, anti-family political movement that encourages women to leave their husbands, kill their children, practice witchcraft, destroy capitalism and become lesbians.

—*Pat Robertson 1995*

Never before in our history have so many voices clamored to speak in the name of The Family. As the millennium approaches, the rhet-

oric of family values has become ubiquitous, often histrionic, sometimes ludicrous. In November of 1995, Republican Speaker of the
U.S. House of Representatives Newt Gingrich blamed a grisly
crime—the murder of a pregnant woman and the surgical abduc-
tion from her uterus of her healthy unborn baby—on a collapse of
family values that welfare dependency fostered.[1] Corporations and
lobbyists now commonly chant a family-values mantra, often in forms
that defy parody. "The trendiest perfumes of the current era," according to a New York Times style commentator, are "family values
in a bottle—olfactory comfort foods, ripe with the scent-memory of
childhood, redolent of the sweet smells of mother's kitchen."[2] Even
more cynically, "Family values, You have yours! We have ours!"
proclaims a prominent ad for handguns in Gun World. "At Para-
Ordnance we respect family values—yours and ours. All members of
our pistol family share these same values. . . . Get to know our entire
family."[3]

In the name of our democracy, as well as our families, this book
seeks to examine and challenge the rhetoric and politics of family
values. Before I tackle this unfashionable task, I wish to underscore
the fact that I, like many whose views I will criticize, am seriously
troubled by the current state of our families. Indisputably, family life
in the United States today, as in most of the world, is deeply vulnerable and insecure. The past four decades have yanked the rug out
from under patterns of family, work, and sexuality that most Westerners have taken for granted for more than a century, and this
disruption has caused genuine distress—both economic and emotional—in too many lives. The uncertainty principle that now governs our work lives—who will have employment, for how long, and
with what risks and rewards?—also governs our most intimate relationships, severely disrupting domestic tranquility and seeding nostalgia for those better times which The Family has come to
symbolize. Without question, there is reason aplenty to harbor concerns for the health, safety, and welfare of our nation's families. From
this perspective, the contemporary appeal of family-values parlance is
quite easy to comprehend.

Nonetheless, I believe it is crucial to recognize that moralistic rhetoric deployed in the name of The Family has been fueling politics that harm rather than help actual families and that impair the social fabric upon which all families depend. Backlash sentiment against the dramatic family transformations of the past four decades has played an increasingly pivotal role in national politics in the United States since the late 1970s, when the divorce rate peaked, and a national White House Conference on The Family that was planned during the Carter administration fractured into three, deeply polarized, regional conferences on families convened during the first year of the Reagan administration. The Moral Majority and profamily movements of the Christian right established the grass-roots base for the Reagan-Bush era. These forces have successfully transformed the Republican Party into an anti-feminist, anti-gay, anti-abortion fortress where "moderate" candidates, such as Senators Arlen Specter and Pete Wilson, who fail any of these litmus tests, cannot seriously contend for their party's presidential nomination. Not even those appointed to Republican staff positions, like Robert Dole's chief-of-staff, Sheila Burke, are safe from the right-wing family-values police. The Christian right has been actively working to drive Burke, who is pro-choice, from office. Heritage Foundation founder Paul Weyrich calls her "a feminist who has mastered the art of manipulating the Senate majority leader." During a debate over the preamble to the welfare bill, Burke sided with those who wished to define marriage as "*a* foundation of society" rather than "*the* foundation" as conservatives insisted. "There are other parts of society—you know, celibate priests—who are important," Burke, who is a Catholic, observed. The opposing camp prevailed, however, and when the quarrel made the papers, the victorious conservatives portrayed Burke as having taken sides with single mothers and homosexuals. "It was translated into my hating marriage," she explained.[4]

The election to the presidency of Democrat Bill Clinton in 1992 seemed to promise a shift in national political rhetoric and policy. Premised on the slogan, "it's the economy, stupid," Clinton's 1992 presidential campaign had affirmed tolerance and support for diverse kinds of families. But startlingly soon after his election, Clinton too jumped on the family-values trolley. Republicans and Democrats alike now compete to promote their politics in the name of the family—meaning one particular kind of family. Jobs programs and health insurance reforms—changes that might have provided desperately needed tangible relief to vast numbers of actual and potential families—suffered catastrophic defeat after Clinton took office in 1993. Meanwhile, both parties employed family-values rhetoric to rationalize dismantling the welfare state and shifting budget priorities from schools, social services, and crime prevention programs to prisons and police. Legislators claimed that "two tykes and you're out" caps on eligibility for welfare benefits would reduce rates of "illegitimacy" and decrease the numbers of single-mother families that they blame for the rising numbers of criminals in the United States.

In the name of The Family, legislators justify terminating public support for the arts, humanities research, and public broadcasting. They claim that artists like deceased gay photographer Robert Mapplethorpe subject the young to corrosive sexual images and ideas, an affront compounded by publicly funded scholars, critics and journalists who canonize and disseminate such work. Likewise, journalists characterize government assaults on free speech, such as a bill passed by both the U.S. House and Senate in December 1995 to impose fines up to $100,000 and prison terms up to five years for people who make "indecent" material available to minors on computer networks, as "a victory by 'family values' Republicans."[5] Family-values rhetoric helped to defeat Clinton's attempt to integrate gays openly into the military. It is being deployed to prevent sex education, the distribution of contraceptives to teen-agers, and access to abortion. And, of course, family-values rhetoric served as a key idiom for the *Contract with America* which Gingrich and his Republican colleagues used to rout their Democratic opponents in 1994. The preamble to their contract offered voters "a Congress that respects the values and shares the faith of the American family," a principle the candidates promised to demonstrate during the first 100 days of the 104th Congress by introducing both the "Personal Responsibility Act," designed to "discourage illegitimacy and teen pregnancy," and the "Family Reinforcement Act," to promote "the central role of families in American society."[6] Pitifully few voices now can be heard in dissent. Thirty years ago, Daniel Patrick Moynihan initiated late twentieth-century moralistic discourse on family values in the United States when he depicted black single-mother families as a "tangle of pathology." At that time, most African-Americans denounced Moynihan for blaming the victim and for imposing a narrow definition of legitimate family structure on a heterogeneous population. Yet many of the same blacks cast a symbolic vote for just this definition of family values when they joined the Million Man March on Oct 16, 1995 that Louis Farrakhan called to inspire black men to take their proper place at the "head of families" and as "maintainers" of women and children. (Black women, meanwhile, were advised to "stay at home" in order to show their support.)[7] Likewise, even flagship organs of the scorned, liberal "cultural elite" like the *Atlantic* monthly now often march in tune by featuring stories that praise Dan Quayle's attack on unwed mothers, or express reservations about sex education, or raise ethical qualms over allowing lesbians and other unmarried women access to sperm banks.

Even many liberal scholars who were once highly critical of 1950s family mores have been falling in line. For example, historian Edward Shorter, whose 1975 book *The Making of the Modern Family* first used the term "the postmodern family," now asks, "What happened? How did the sugar-plum visions of postmodernity of 1975 turn into the nightmare specter of 1995?"[8] It pains me to think that the new Republican majority might be on the side of the angels," Shorter confesses,

> but when Newt Gingrich and friends say they want to repeal the counterculture, at least a part of what they have in mind is arresting and

reversing the social trends that have undermined the modern family—
specifically, the collective ideology of "rights" and the personal strategy
of "entitlement." The notion of rights, as it plays out within the family,
is antithetical to a sense of commonweal, in which individuals often
have to subordinate their needs and wishes so that the collectivity may
thrive.[9]

Betraying a good deal of conceptual confusion, scholars, politicians and citizens anxiously debate whether or not "the family" will
survive the twentieth century at all. Of course, anxieties like these are
hardly new. "For at least 150 years," as historian Linda Gordon has
noted, "there have been periods of fear that 'the family'—meaning a
popular image of what families were supposed to be like, by no
means a correct recollection of any actual 'traditional' family—was
in decline; and these fears have tended to escalate in periods of social
stress."[10] The actual subject of this recurring, fretful discourse is a
specific form of family life, one that historians like Shorter call the
"modern" family. No doubt, we who write about family change this
way have not abetted public understanding by using the concept of
the modern family to designate a family form that most Americans
now consider to be traditional—an intact nuclear unit inhabited by
a male breadwinner, his full-time homemaker wife, and their dependent children. For this "modern" family is precisely the form that
many today mistake for an ancient, essential, and now-endangered
institution.

The past half-century of postindustrial social and economic transformations in the United States and Europe have rung down the
historic curtain on the modern family regime. In 1950, three-fifths of
U.S. households contained a male breadwinner and a full-time female homemaker, whether children resided with the couples or
not.[11] Now, more than three-fifths of married women with dependent children are in the labor force, as well as a majority of mothers
of infants, while there are more than twice as many single-mother
families as married, homemaker-mom families.[12] By the middle of

the 1970s, moreover, divorce had outstripped death as the key source of marital dissolutions, generating in its wake a complex array of new kinship ties and tribulations. While here too the United States leads most of the globe, the same demographic and social trends pervade the postindustrial world. The diversity of our contemporary kinship relationships undermines Tolstoy's famous contrast between happy and unhappy families: even happy families no longer are all alike.[13] No longer is there a single culturally dominant family pattern, like the "modern" one, to which a majority of citizens conform and most of the rest aspire. Instead, postindustrial conditions have compelled and encouraged us to craft a wide array of family arrangements which we inhabit uneasily and reconstitute frequently as our occupational and personal circumstances shift.

We have been living through a tumultuous and fractious period of family history, a period after the modern family order, but before what we cannot foretell. When Shorter employed the term "the postmodern family" in 1975, he did so to underscore three emergent trends of Western family life that he considered unprecedented— peer influence surpassing parental influence over the young, marital instability, and women's departure from the nest.[14] Although I agree that these are important features of contemporary family life, I use the term postmodern family instead to signal the contested, ambivalent, and undecided character of our contemporary family cultures. The postmodern, as art historian Clive Dilnot has suggested, "is first, an uncertainty, an insecurity, a doubt." Most of the "post" words provoke uneasiness because they imply "both the end, or at least the radical transformation, of a familiar pattern of activity or group of ideas," and the emergence of "new fields of cultural activity whose contours are still unclear and whose meanings and implications . . . cannot yet be fathomed."[15]

Like postmodern culture, contemporary Western family arrangements are diverse, fluid, and unresolved. Like postmodern cultural forms, our families today admix unlikely elements in an improvisational pastiche of old and new. The postmodern family condition is not a new model of family life equivalent to that of the modern family; it is not the next stage in an orderly progression of stages of family history; rather the postmodern family condition signals the moment in that history when our belief in a logical progression of stages has broken down. Modernization narratives about "the family," like the one in Shorter's *The Making of the Modern Family*, once portrayed Western family life steadily evolving toward a more democratic and progressive form. Rupturing this self-congratulatory and reassuring logic, the postmodern family condition incorporates both experimental and nostalgic dimensions as it lurches forward and backward into an uncertain future.

In 1990, I published *Brave New Families*, a book about this postmodern family condition that was based upon three years of fieldwork I had conducted during the height of the Reagan-Bush era among (not always) working people in California's Silicon Valley.[16] *Brave New Families* depicts people struggling heroically and creatively, but with mixed success, to navigate the new gender, family and work conditions of postindustrial dislocations. Two years after its publication, defenders of "family values" attacked my book in the pages of the *New York Times* and elsewhere, portraying (in my view, misportraying) it as uncritically celebrating the postmodern family condition and an "anything goes" approach to family life. Social scientists James Q. Wilson and David Popenoe both identified my stance with the misguided school of "family optimism, since it stresses that changes in the contemporary family are really nothing to worry about." More pointedly, the late historian Christopher Lasch chided me for feminist "ideological preconceptions" that produced "cheery conclusions" to which "Stacey's research does not lend much support."[17]

Those attacks first inspired this book in which I try not to respond defensively to such tendentious readings of *Brave New Families* in order to set the record straight, but rather to move public discussion beyond the polarized pieties of moralistic rhetoric toward more substantive, and more moral, political responses to our common plight.

Laissez-faire standards never have characterized my personal family practices nor politics. Postmodern family changes *are* threatening and ambivalent, as I had imagined the portraits of the families conveyed in *Brave New Families* made clear. It is true that I believe that postmodern changes in work, family, and sexual opportunities for women and men do open the prospect of introducing greater democracy, equality and choice than ever before into our most intimate relationships, especially for women and members of sexual minorities. However, I am likewise well aware that this democratic potential carries a big-ticket price tag of endemic instability and uncertainty. Unfortunately, for reasons I will discuss, more people have been paying the price than have been receiving fair value in the transaction.

It is unsurprising, therefore, that so many today indulge fantasies of "escaping" from freedom and succumb to the alluring certainties of family-values pieties. But there are also elements of bad faith in popular nostalgia for modern, breadwinner-homemaker nuclear family life. If we judge mainstream family values more by what people do than by what they say about their family lives, we will find little evidence that most Americans genuinely wish to return to the gender order that those domestic sitcom families of the 1950s, like "Ozzie and Harriet," have come to symbolize. Voting with their hearts and deeds rather than their words and creeds, the vast majority of Americans have been actively remaking their family lives, and their expectations about family life as well. For example, by a ratio of three to one, people surveyed in a 1990 *Newsweek* poll defined the family as "a group of people who love and care for each other" (quite a postmodern definition), rather than by the legalistic definition of "a group of people related by blood, marriage, or adoption." And while a majority of those surveyed gave negative ratings to the quality of American family life in general, 71 percent declared themselves "at least very satisfied" with their own family lives.[18] Moreover, a *New York Times* survey in 1989 found that more than two-thirds of women, including a majority of those living in "traditional" (that is to say "modern") male breadwinner-female homemaker households, as well as a majority of men agreed that, "the United States continues to need a strong women's movement to push for changes that benefit women."[19]

Little wonder so many politicians whose professed family values prove to be blatantly hypocritical find it easy to exploit this popular bad faith. House Speaker Newt Gingrich is a prime example. He pledged to reform the "very destructive" work pace of Congress because, he claimed, it "brutalizes and damages families." Yet, the same Gingrich dictated harsh divorce terms to his first wife while she was in the hospital with cancer so that he could marry his second, younger one; he also held the Congress in session long into the 1995 Christmas holiday recess period (while many government workers angrily endured an unpaid furlough) during a partisan stalemate with the president, who had threatened to veto budget cuts that guaranteed disaster for indigent families. Ironically, under Gingrich, the Congressional schedule has become so brutal and damaging to families that one Republican congressman claims members find themselves forced to "raise children by memo," and marriages quickly began to crumble within the ranks of the celebrated, conservative freshman congressional class of '95. Among the most prominent and embarrassing of these failing marriages was that of conservative freshwoman star Enid Woldholtz of Utah, who campaigned on the basis of her skills as a corporate lawyer and on a family-values platform, but quickly filed divorce papers against her husband (who was also her campaign financial manager) and portrayed herself teary-eyed on national TV as a gullible, ignorant, wronged wife, amid charges of gross campaign finance improprieties.[20]

The contrast between the family lives many of us forge and those we claim to esteem, like the discrepant assessments people give of their own families and those in the nation as a whole, hint at how reluctant many are to fully own up to the genuine ambivalence we feel about contemporary family and social change. Yet ambivalence, as sociologist Alan Wolfe suggests, is an underappreciated, but responsible, moral stance, and one ideally suited for democratic citizenship: "Given the paradoxes of modernity [and even more so of postmodernity, I would add], there is little wrong, and perhaps a great deal right, with being ambivalent—especially when there is so much to be ambivalent about."[21]

More to the point, perhaps, whatever our "real" family values may actually be, we cannot rewind the historical reel in a quest to escape postmodern family life, however much some might wish to do so. "This is what is going on now," as single mother and author Shoshana Alexander sensibly reminds us. "This is what our families are like now."[22] Therefore, we have only two real choices. Either we can come to grips with the postmodern family condition by accepting the end of a singular ideal family and begin to promote better living and spiritual conditions for the diverse array of real families we actually inhabit and desire. Or we can continue to engage in denial, resistance, displacement, and bad faith, by cleaving to a moralistic ideology of *the family* at the same time that we fail to provide social and economic conditions that make life for the modern family or any other kind of family viable, let alone dignified and secure.

·   ·   ·

A comparative perspective on global family change could be quite useful here. The most cursory cross-national glance reveals that the postmodern family condition is endemic to all postindustrial nations in the era of global capitalism, but that national responses to its challenges, and therefore its human consequences, vary considerably. In the Scandinavian nations, for example, social democratic policies continue to enjoy much greater popularity than family-values rhetoric. Consequently, even though Scandinavian marriage rates are far lower than in the United States, and unwed motherhood is much less stigmatized, nonetheless teen pregnancy and child poverty are practically unknown. Moreover, contrary to popular belief, suicide rates for youth in Sweden are much lower than they are in the United States, Switzerland, Canada, Australia, Germany, or even Japan—all countries with much more conservative family rhetoric and policies.[23] This suggests that the collective challenge that citizens of postindustrial societies must confront is to accept, if we cannot embrace, the reality of family diversity and flux with as much grace, wisdom, tolerance and compassion as we can muster. Otherwise, we must resign ourselves to ceaseless family-values wars that encourage policies destructive to most real families of all kinds.

As an aging, second-wave, progressive feminist—a bit sadder and less hopeful, perhaps, than when I wrote *Brave New Families*, but unrepentant—I write this book to urge that we choose the former course. I remain committed to seizing whatever democratic opportunities the postmodern family condition offers us for basing our family ties on a minimum of coercion, inequality, and prescribed forms of gender, sexuality, or kinship. Still, we must entertain no illusions that truly democratic principles of family life will be easy to achieve, practice, or sustain. Even if we could achieve consensus on such an ideal, we would never attain perfect familial peace or nirvana. But so too is democracy a threatening, ambivalent, imperfect political regime that few, if any, peoples in history have been able to practice or sustain without turmoil, conflict, struggle, or grief. Such are the burdens of freedom.

The challenge of postmodernity, as of democracy, is to learn to live with instability and flux as responsibly, ethically and humanely as possible. To do so we must cultivate individual resilience, flexibility, courage, and tolerance while we work collectively to provide the best forms of social and cultural supports we can devise to cushion the inevitable disruptions and disappointments, the hardships and heartaches, that all families and humans must inevitably confront.

The chapters that follow depict and interpret the sources and consequences of the second American family revolution—the shift from the modern to the postmodern family regime and the family values wars that this revolution has unleashed. Like African-American legal scholar Patricia Williams, who responded with plaintive eloquence to the 1995 Million Man March of African-American men in an essay titled, "Different Drummer Please, Marchers!,"[24] I want to urge family-values enthusiasts to accustom their ears to more cosmopolitan, world beat, feminist and democratic family rhythms. I try to resist all moralistic platitudes, mantras, and dogmas about family values, irrespective of their political labels. I hope to disrupt the aura of false consensus on family values that permeates our culture by exposing flaws in the research assumptions, evidence, and logic upon which it is based. I challenge widespread misconceptions about the current status of social science research on family change and about the relationships between family politics and the politics of gender, race, sexuality, and welfare. I seek to clarify distinctions between family and social "diseases," and between problems associated with the structure and the quality of our family ties.

This book takes issue with ubiquitous claims that family breakdown is the principal source of most of what's wrong with our society today, such as those offered in the epigraphs by Illinois' Governor Edgar and California's Governor Wilson. I challenge both the math and the sociology behind Governor Edgar's estimate that the source of 80 percent of the problems that cross his desk can be traced to family breakdown. While neither of us is a quantitative social scientist, my more empirically informed, armchair estimates are almost the inverse of his. To paraphrase the governor loosely: "As a family sociologist, I can tell you that about 70 percent of the problems that hit my desk you can trace back to the breakdown of the economic and social structure in our society (the other 30 percent are probably indelible features of the human condition), and I think anyone who doesn't want to admit that is not only kidding themselves (sic)," but also is shirking a personal portion of our collective responsibility in the name of The Family. Thus, I also challenge the social logic and statistics supporting the claim by the governor of my own state, Pete Wilson, that "a child's future will really be determined by just two villagers—mom and dad." In the complex, interdependent, "global village" we now inhabit, few if any villagers can control the kinds of resources, cultural influences, opportunities, dangers and rewards that will determine their children's fate. It now takes much more than a village to help a child become a responsible, competent, and ethical adult, or even to survive the passage.

. . . .

The individual chapters of this book, like the postmodern family condition they analyze, can be read in a variety of combinations. Because several were first written as discrete essays, each chapter can stand on its own, but each also pays its respects to its forebears and enriches its neighbors, just as I would wish our diverse family cultures might do. The first two chapters portray the general features of the postmodern family condition in North America and Europe. Chapter one, "Backward toward the Postmodern Family," distills a synopsis of the ethnographic research I presented in *Brave New Families* in order to challenge the popular view that an affluent or middle-class "cultural elite" spearheaded most of the prominent features of contemporary family life. It depicts the unintended origins and contradictory character of postmodern kinship strategies among working people struggling to get by and move on. The second chapter, "The Family Is Dead; Long Live Our Families," which was inspired by the United Nations declaration of 1994 as the International Year of The Family, situates the general condition of postmodern kinship in its broader historical and international context. It also provides an introduction to and critique of mainstream social science theories about the development and diffusion of the modern family system.

The next two chapters treat an unanticipated secular campaign for family values that has flourished in the media and inside the beltway during the Clinton administration. Chapter three, "The Neo-Family Values Campaign," describes the institutional networks responsible for organizing this centrist campaign and for achieving remarkable influence over the Democratic administration and the mainstream, and even liberal, media. It also offers a critical analysis of the social science arguments and the political rhetoric the campaign has deployed to convince the president and public to subscribe to the same family breakdown sociology thesis that governors Edgar and Wilson both promote. In particular, chapter three decodes the hidden injuries of the racial, economic, gender and sexual meanings that pious family-values rhetoric conveys in veiled guise and argues that in the name of The Family, the rights and interests of African-Americans, the poor, women, and gays and lesbians are endangered. Chapter four, "Virtual Social Science and the Politics of Family Values," steps further back from the fray to explore shifts in the politics of knowledge inside and outside the academy that helped to generate this unexpected, and in my view unfortunate, collaborative effort by mainstream politicians and social scientists to affix public attention on fifties sitcom family values. It also discusses the paradoxical impact feminism has had both on social science and on family politics in the United States.

Finally, chapter five, "Gay and Lesbian Families Are Here; All Our Families Are Queer; Let's Get Used to It!," encourages us to move forward, rather than backward, toward postmodern family life. I conclude this book with an extensive analysis of gay and lesbian families, because I take them to be neither marginal nor exceptional, but rather to represent a paradigmatic illustration of the "queer" postmodern conditions of kinship that we all now inhabit. Gays and lesbians who self consciously form families are forced to confront the challenges, opportunities and dilemmas of the postmodern condition with much lower levels of denial, resistance, displacement or bad faith than most others can indulge. "Free"—or perhaps bereft—of the restrictions and benefits that prescribed forms of kinship confer, they creatively devise a host of diverse forms of their own. *This is what is going on now.* If the rest of us could only "get used to it," the experiments and experiences of gay families might serve as instructional models of postmodern family challenges, ingenuity, variety and courage — ones from which all contemporary families and communities could learn and benefit. Perhaps their example could inspire others to accept the burdens, the paradoxes and the possibilities of "what our families are like now." In the name of all of our families, I have written this book with such a vision in mind.

CHAPTER 1

Backward toward the
Postmodern Family

. . . .

The extended family is in our lives again. This should make all
the people happy who were complaining back in the sixties and
seventies that the reason family life was so hard, especially on
mothers, was that the nuclear family had replaced the extended
family. . . . Your basic extended family today includes your ex-
husband or -wife, your ex's new mate, your new mate, possibly
your new mate's ex, and any new mate that your new mate's ex
has acquired. It consists entirely of people who are not related
by blood, many of whom can't stand each other. This return of
the extended family reminds me of the favorite saying of my
friend's extremely pessimistic mother: Be careful what you wish
for, you might get it.

Delia Ephron, Funny Sauce

In the summer of 1986 I attended a wedding ceremony in a small
Christian pentecostal church in the Silicon Valley. The service celebrated the same "traditional" family patterns and values that two

years earlier had inspired a profamily movement to assist Ronald Reagan's landslide reelection to the presidency of the United States. At the same time, however, the pastor's rhetoric displayed substantial sympathy with feminist criticisms of patriarchal marriage. "A ring is not a shackle, and marriage is not a relationship of domination," he instructed the groom. Moreover, the complex patterns of divorce, remarriage, and stepkinship that linked the members of the wedding party and their guests bore far greater resemblance to the New Age extended family satirized by Delia Ephron than they did to the image of traditional family life which arouses widespread nostalgic fantasies among religious and other social critics of contemporary family practices. Serving as the wedding photographer was the bride's former husband accompanied by his live-in lover, a Jewish divorcee who hoped to become his third wife. All of the wedding attendants were stepkin or step-in-laws to the groom: two daughters from the bride's first marriage served as their mother's bride matrons; their brother joined one daughter's second husband as ushers for the groom; and the proud flower girl was a young granddaughter from the bride matron's first marriage. At least half the pews were filled with members of four generations from the confusing tangle of former, step-, dual, and in-law relatives of this postmodern, divorce-extended family.

Family Revolutions and Vanguard Classes

Two centuries ago leading white, middle-class families in the newly united American states spearheaded a family revolution that gradually replaced the diversity and fluidity of the premodern domestic order with a more uniform modern family system.[1] But "modern family" was an oxymoronic label for this peculiar institution that dispensed modernity to white, middle-class men only by withholding it from women. Men could enter the public sphere as breadwinners and citizens, because their wives were confined to the newly privatized family realm. Ruled by an increasingly absent patriarchal landlord, the modern middle-class family, a woman's domain, soon was sentimentalized as "traditional."

It took most of the subsequent two centuries for substantial numbers of white working-class men to achieve the rudimentary economic passbook to modern family life—a male family wage.[2] By the time they had done so, however, a second family revolution was well underway. Once again, middle-class, white families appeared to be in the forefront. This time women were claiming the benefits and burdens of modernity, a status that could be achieved only at the expense of the "modern" family itself. Reviving a long-dormant feminist movement, frustrated middle-class homemakers and their more militant daughters subjected modern domesticity to a sustained critique, at times with little sensitivity to the effects our anti-modern family ideology might have on women for whom full-time domesticity had rarely been feasible. Thus, feminist family reform came to be regarded widely as a white middle-class agenda, and white, working-class families its most resistant adversaries.

I shared these presumptions before conducting fieldwork among families in Santa Clara County, California—the "Silicon Valley"—during the mid-1980s. This radically altered my understanding of the class basis of the postmodern family revolution. Once a bucolic agribusiness orchard region, during the 1960s and 1970s this county became the global headquarters of the electronics industry and the world's vanguard postindustrial region. While economic restructuring commanded global attention, most outside observers overlooked the concurrent gender and family changes that preoccupied many Silicon Valley residents. During the late 1970s, before the conservative shift in the national political climate made feminism a derogatory term, local public officials proudly described San Jose, the county seat, as a feminist capital. The city elected a feminist mayor and hosted the statewide NOW convention in 1974. Santa Clara County soon became one of the first counties in the nation to elect a female majority to its Board of Supervisors. In 1981, high levels of feminist activism made San Jose the site of the nation's first successful strike for a comparable worth standard of pay for city employees.[3]

During its postindustrial makeover, the Silicon Valley also became an avant garde region for family change, where family and household data represented an exaggeration of national trends. For example, while the national divorce rate was doubling after 1960, in Santa Clara County it nearly tripled. "Non-family" and single-parent households grew faster than in the rest of the nation, and abortion rates were one and one-half the national figures.[4] The high marriage casualty rate among workaholic engineers was dubbed "the silicon syndrome,"[5] and many residents shared an alarmist view of family life captured in the opening lines of an article in a local university magazine: "There is an endangered species in Silicon Valley, one so precious that when it disappears Silicon Valley will die with it. This endangered species is the family. And sometimes it seems as if every institution in this valley—political, corporate, and social—is hellbent on driving it into extinction."[6]

The coincidence of epochal changes in occupational, gender, and family patterns made the Silicon Valley a propitious site for exploring ways in which ordinary working people had been remaking their families in the wake of postindustrial and feminist challenges. The Silicon Valley is by no means a typical or representative U.S. location, but because national postindustrial work and family transformations were more condensed, rapid, and exaggerated there than elsewhere, they were easier to perceive. Most of the popular and scholarly literature about white, working-class people, on the other hand, portrays them as the most traditional, as the last bastion of the modern family. Relatively privileged members of the white working class especially were widely regarded as the bulwark of the Reagan revolution and the constituency least sympathetic to feminism and family reforms. Those whose hold on the accoutrements of the American Dream was so recent and tenuous, it was thought, had the strongest incentives to defend it.[7]

For nearly three years, between the summer of 1984 and the

spring of 1987, I conducted a commuter fieldwork study of two
tended kin networks composed primarily of white, working peo₁
who had resided in Santa Clara County throughout the period of its
startling transformation. My research convinced me that white,
middle-class families were less the innovators than the propagandists
and principal beneficiaries of contemporary family change.

Remaking Family Life in the Silicon Valley

Two challenges to my class and gender prejudices provoked my turn
to ethnographic research and the selection of the two kin groups who
became its focus. Pamela Gama[8], an administrator of social services
for women at a Silicon Valley anti-poverty agency when I met her in
July of 1984, became central to my study when she challenged my
secular feminist preconceptions by "coming out" to me as a recent
born-again Christian convert. Pamela was the 47-year-old bride at the
Christian wedding ceremony I attended two years later. There she
exchanged vows with her second husband, Albert Gama, a construction worker, with whom she had previously cohabited. Pamela's first
marriage in 1960 to Don Franklin, the father of her three children,
lasted fifteen years, spanning the headiest days of Silicon Valley
development and the period of Don's successful rise from telephone
repairman to electronics packaging engineer.

In contrast, Dotty Lewison, my central contact in the second kin
network I studied, challenged my class prejudices. The physical appearance and appurtenances of the worn and modest Lewison abode,
Dotty's polyester attire and bawdy speech, her husband's heavily
tattooed body, and the geographic and occupational details of her
family's history satisfied all of my stereotypic notions of an authentic
working-class family. But the history of feminist activism Dotty re-
counted proudly, as she unpacked a newly purchased bible, demonstrated the serious limitations of my tacit understandings. When I
met Dotty in October of 1984, she was the veteran of an intact and
reformed marriage of thirty years' duration to her disabled husband,

Lou, formerly an electronics maintenance mechanic and supervisor, as well as, I would later learn, a wife and child abuser.

Pamela, Dotty, and several of their friends whom I came to know during my study were members of Betty Friedan's *Feminine Mystique* generation, but not of her social class. Unlike the more affluent members of Friedan's intended audience, Pam and Dotty were "beneficiaries" of the late, ephemeral achievement of a male family wage and homeownership won by privileged sectors of the working class. This was a pyrrhic victory, as it turned out, that had allowed this population a brief period of access to the modern family system just as it was decomposing. Pam and Dotty, like most white women of their generation, were young when they married in the 1950s and early 1960s. They entered their first marriages with gender expectations about family and work responsibilities that were conventional for their era. For a significant period of time, they and their husbands conformed, as best they could, to the culturally prescribed pattern of male breadwinner and female homemaker. Assuming primary responsibility for rearing the children they began to bear immediately after marriage, Pam and Dotty supported their husbands' successful efforts to progress from working-class to middle- and upper-middle-class careers in the electronics industry. Their experiences with the modern family, however, were always more tenuous, less pure, than those women to whom, and for whom, Betty Friedan spoke.

The insecurities and inadequacies of their husbands' earnings made itinerant labor force participation by Dotty and Pam both necessary and resented by their husbands before feminism made female employment a badge of pride. Dotty alternated frequent childbearing with recurrent forays into the labor force in a wide array of low-wage jobs. In fact, Dotty herself assembled semiconductors before her husband, Lou, entered the electronics industry, but she did not perceive or desire significant opportunities for her own occupational mobility at that point. Pamela's husband began his career ascent earlier than Dotty's, but Pamela still found his earnings insufficient, and his spending habits too profligate, to balance the household budget. To make the ends of their beyond-their-means, middle-class lifestyle meet without undermining her husband's pride, Pam shared childcare and a clandestine housecleaning occupation with her African-American neighbor and friend, Lorraine. Thus Pam and Dotty did not manage to suffer the full effects of what Friedan had termed the "problem without a name" until feminism had begun to name it, and in terms both women found compelling.

In the early 1970s, while their workaholic husbands were increasingly absent from their families, Pam and Dotty each joined friends taking women's reentry courses in local community colleges. There they encountered feminism, and their lives and their modern families were never the same. Feminism provided an analysis and rhetoric for their discontent, and it helped each develop the self-esteem she needed to exit or reform her unhappy modern marriage. Both women left their husbands, became welfare mothers and experimented with the single life. Pam divorced, pursued a college degree, and developed a social service career. Dotty, with lesser educational credentials and employment options, took her husband back, but on her own terms, after his disabling heart attack (and after a lover left her). Disabled, Lou ceased his physical abuse and performed most of the housework, while Dotty had control over her time, some of which she devoted to community activism in anti-battering work.

By the time I met Pamela and Dotty a decade later, at a time when my own feminist-inspired joint household of the prior eight years was failing, national and local feminist ardor had cooled. Pam was then a recent convert to born-again Christianity, receiving Christian marriage counseling to buttress and enhance her second marriage to construction worker Al. Certainly this represented a retreat from feminist family ideology, but, as Pamela gradually taught me, a far less dramatic retreat than I at first imagined.[9] Like other women active in the contemporary evangelical Christian revival, Pam was making creative use of its surprisingly flexible patriarchal ideology to reform her husband in her own image. She judged it "not so bad a deal" to cede Al nominal family headship in exchange for substantial improvements in his conjugal behavior. Indeed, few contemporary feminists would find fault with the Christian marital principles that Al identified as his goals: "I just hope that we can come closer together and be more honest with each other. Try to use God as a guideline. The goals are more openness, a closer relationship, be more loving both verbally and physically, have more concern for the other person's feelings."

Nor did Pamela's conversion return her to a modern family pattern. Instead she collaborated with her first husband's live-in Jewish lover, Shirley Moskowitz, to build a remarkably harmonious and inclusive divorce-extended kin network whose constituent households swapped resources, labor, and lodgers in response to shifting family circumstances and needs.

Dotty Lewison was also no longer a political activist when we met in 1984. Instead she was supplementing Lou's disability pension with part-time paid work in a small insurance office and pursuing spiritual exploration more overtly postmodern in form than Pam's in a metaphysical Christian church. During the course of my fieldwork, however, an overwhelming series of tragedies claimed the lives of Dotty's husband and two of the Lewisons' five adult children. Dotty successfully contested her abusive son-in-law for custody of her four motherless grandchildren. Struggling to support them, she formed a joint household with her only occupationally successful child, Kristina, an electronics drafter-designer and a single mother of one child. While Dotty and Pamela both had moved partway back from feminist fervor, at the same time both had moved further away from the (no-longer) modern family.

Between them, Pamela and Dotty had eight children—five daughters and three sons—children of modern families disrupted by postindustrial developments and feminist challenges. All were in their twenties when I first met them in 1984 and 1985, members of the quintessential postfeminist generation. Although all five daughters distanced themselves from feminist identity and ideology, all too had semiconsciously incorporated feminist principles into their gender and kin expectations and practices. They took for granted, and, at times eschewed, the gains in women's work opportunities, sexual autonomy and male participation in childrearing and domestic work for which feminists of their mothers' generation struggled. Ignorant or disdainful of the political efforts feminists had expended to secure such gains, they were preoccupied instead coping with the expanded opportunities and burdens women now encounter. They came of age in a period that expected a successful woman to combine marriage to a communicative, egalitarian man with motherhood and an engaging, rewarding career. All but one of these daughters of successful white working-class fathers had absorbed these postfeminist expectations, the firstborns most fully. Yet none found such a pattern attainable. Only Pam's younger daughter, Katie, the original source of the evangelical conversions in her own marriage and her mother's, explicitly rejected such a vision. At fourteen, Katie joined the Christian revival, where, I believe, she found an effective refuge from the disruptions of parental divorce and adolescent drug culture that had threatened her more rebellious siblings. Ironically, however, Katie's total involvement in a Pentecostal ministry led her to practice the most alternative family arrangement of all. Katie, with her husband and young children, lived "in community" in various joint households (occasionally interracial households) whose accordian structures and shared childrearing, ministry labors, and expenses enabled her to integrate her family, work, and spiritual life to an exceptional, and enviable, degree.

At the outset of my fieldwork, none of Pam's or Dotty's daughters inhabited a modern family. However, over the next few years, discouraging experiences with the jobs available to them led three to retreat from the world of paid work and to attempt a modified version of the modern family strategy that their mothers had practiced earlier. All demanded, and two received, substantially greater male involvement in childcare and domestic work than had their mothers (or mine) in the prefeminist past. Only one, however, seemed to have reasonable prospects for succeeding in her modern gender strategy, and these she had secured through unacknowledged benefits feminism helped her to enjoy. Dotty's second daughter, Polly, had left the Silicon Valley when the electronics company she worked for opened a branch in a state with lower labor and housing costs. Legalized abortion and liberalized sexual norms for women allowed Polly to become heterosexually active while deferring marriage and childbearing until she was able to negotiate a marriage whose domestic labor arrangements represented a distinct improvement over that of the prefeminist modern family. Nonetheless, Polly scorned feminism and political activism.

I have less to say, and less confidence in what I do have to say, about postmodern family strategies among the men in Pam's and Dotty's kin groups. Despite concerted efforts to conduct my research in gender-inclusive terms, the men in the families I studied remained comparatively secondary to my research. In part, this is unavoidable for anyone who attempts to study gender in a gendered world. Being a woman inhibited my access to, and likely my empathy with, the complete range of male family experience. Still, the relative marginality of men in my research was not simply due to methodological deficiencies. It also accurately reflects their more marginal participation in contemporary family life. Most of the men in Pam's and Dotty's networks narrated gender and kinship stories that were relatively inarticulate and undeveloped because they had less experience, investment, or interest in the work of sustaining kin ties.[10]

While economic pressures have always encouraged expansionary kin work among working-class women, these have often weakened men's family ties. Men's muted family voices whisper of a masculinity crisis among blue-collar men. As working-class men's access to breadwinner status has receded, so too has their confidence in their masculinity.[11] The decline of the family wage and the escalation of women's involvement in paid work has generated profound ambivalence about the eroding breadwinner ethic. Pam's and Dotty's male kin, like many postfeminist men, appeared uncertain whether a man who provides sole support to his family is a hero or a chump. Two avoided domestic commitments entirely, while several embraced these wholeheartedly. Two vacillated between romantic engagements and the unencumbered single life. Too many of the men I met expressed their masculinity in antisocial, self-destructive, and violent forms.

Women continue to strive, meanwhile, as they always have, to buttress and reform their male kin. Responding to the extraordinary diffusion of feminist ideology as well as to sheer overwork, working-class women, like middle-class women, have struggled to transfer some of their domestic burdens to men. My fieldwork led me to believe that they had achieved more success in the daily trenches than some of the research on the politics of housework indicates. Working-class women have had more success, I suspect, than most middle-class women.[12] While only a few of the women in my study expected, or desired, men to perform an equal share of housework and child care, none was willing to exempt men from domestic labor. Almost all of the men I observed or heard about routinely performed domestic tasks that my own blue-collar father and his friends never deigned to contemplate. Some did so with reluctance and resentment, but most did so willingly. Although the division of household labor remains profoundly inequitable, a major gender norm has shifted here.[13]

Farewell to Archie Bunker

Contrary to the popular image of the white working-class as the last repository of old-fashioned, "modern" American family life, I found postmodern family arrangements among blue-collar people in the Silicon Valley that were at least as diverse and innovative as those found within the middle-class. Pundits of postmodern family arrangements, like Delia Ephron, satirize the hostility and competition that afflicts many unwilling relatives in contemporary divorce-extended families. But some working women, like Pamela and Dotty, have found ways to transform divorce from a rupture into a kinship resource, and they are not unique. A study of "ex-familia" among middle-class divorced couples and their parents in the suburbs of San Francisco found one-third sustaining kinship ties with former spouses and their relatives.[14] It seems likely that cooperative, ex-familial relationships are even more prevalent among lower-income groups, where divorce rates are higher and women have far greater experience with, and need for, sustaining cooperative kin ties.[15]

Certainly, the dismantling of welfare state protections and the reprivatizing policies of the postindustrial era have given such women renewed incentives to continue their traditions of active, expansionary kin work. The accordion households and kin ties crafted by Dotty Lewison, by Katie's Christian ministry, and by Pam and Shirley draw more on the maternal-centered kin strategies of poor and working-class people[16] than they do on family reform innovations by the white middle class. Ironically, sociologists have identified a new middle-class social problem—those crowded, rather than empty, nests which are filled with incompletely launched young adults, which have been long familiar to the less privileged, like the Lewisons.[17] Postindustrial conditions have reversed the supply-side, trickle-down trajectory of family change predicted by modernization theorists, who have always portrayed the middle classes as the forerunners of family progress. The diversity and complexity of postmodern family patterns rivals that characteristic of premodern kinship forms.[18]

One glimpses the ironies of class and gender history here. For decades, industrial unions struggled heroically to achieve a socially recognized male breadwinner wage that would allow working-class families to participate in the modern gender order. These struggles, however, contributed to the very cheapening of female labor that later made women workers so attractive to postindustrial employers who became free to operate outside a union context. This, in turn, fostered the massive entry of married women into the workforce that has done so much to undermine the modern family regime.[19] Escalating consumption standards, the expansion of mass collegiate coeducation, and the persistence of high divorce rates then gave more and more women ample cause to invest a portion of their identities in the sphere of paid labor.[20] In retrospect, we can see that middle-class women began to abandon their confinement in the modern family just as working-class women were approaching its access ramps. The former did so, however, only after African-American women and the wives of white, working-class men had pioneered the twentieth-century revolution in women's paid work. As working-class wives took whatever jobs they could find during the catastrophic 1930s, participated in defense industries in the 1940s, and raised their family incomes to middle-class standards by returning to the labor force rapidly after childrearing in the 1950s, they quietly modeled and normalized the postmodern family standard of employment for married mothers. Whereas in 1950 the less a man earned, the more likely his wife was employed, by 1968 it was the wives of middle-income men who were the most likely to be in the labor force.[21]

African-American women have always had to work and to devise alternative, cooperative kin ties in order to sustain their vulnerable families. They and white, working-class women have been the genuine postmodern family pioneers, even though they also suffer the most from its most negative effects. Long denied the mixed benefits that the modern family order offered middle-class women, less privileged women quietly forged alternative models of femininity to full-time domesticity and mother-intensive childrearing. Struggling creatively, often heroically, to sustain oppressed families and to escape the most oppressive ones, they drew on "traditional," premodern kinship resources and crafted untraditional ones. In the process, they created postmodern family strategies.

Rising divorce and cohabitation rates, working mothers, two-earner households, single and unwed parenthood, along with intergenerational female-linked extended kin support networks appeared earlier and more extensively among poor and working-class people.[22] Economic pressures, rather than ideological principles, governed many of these departures from domesticity, but many working women found additional reasons to appreciate paid employment.[23] Eventually white, middle-class women, sated and even sickened by our modern family privileges,[24] began to emulate, elaborate, and celebrate many of these alternative family practices. How ironic and unfortunate it seems, therefore, that feminism's antimodern family ideology should come to offend many women from the social groups whose gender and kinship strategies helped to foster it.

If postindustrial transformations have encouraged modern, working-class families to reorganize and diversify even earlier and more extensively than middle-class families, it seems time to put to rest any notion of *the* working-class family. This concept is deeply androcentric and class-biased, and it distorts the history and the current reality of wage-earning people's intimate relationships. Popular images of working-class family life, like the Archie Bunker family of 1970s TV sitcom fame, rest upon the iconography of unionized, blue-collar, male, industrial breadwinners and the history of their lengthy struggle for the family wage. But the male family wage was a late and ephemeral achievement of only the most fortunate sections of the modern industrial working-class. It is doubtful that most working-class men ever secured access to its patriarchal domestic privileges.

Postmodern conditions have exposed the gendered character of this social-class category, just as they render the category out of date. As feminists have argued, only by disregarding women's labor and learning was it ever plausible to designate a family unit as working class.[25] In an era when most married mothers are employed, when women perform most working-class jobs,[26] when most occupations are unorganized and fail to pay a family wage, when marriage links are tenuous and transitory, and when more single women than married homemakers are rearing children, conventional notions of a normal working-class family no longer make sense. The life circumstances and social mobility patterns of the members of Pamela's kin set and of the Lewisons, for example, were so diverse and fluid that no single social-class category could adequately describe any of the family units among them.

If the white, working-class family stereotype is inaccurate, it is also consequential. Stereotypes are moral (alas, more often, immoral) stories people tell to organize the complexity of social experience. Narrating the working-class as profamily reactionaries suppresses the diversity and the innovative character of a great deal of their kin relationships. A plot with socially divisive and conservative political effects, the Archie Bunker stereotype of working-class families may have helped to contain feminism by estranging middle-class from working-class women. Barbara Ehrenreich has argued that caricatures that portray the working-class as racist and reactionary were self-serving inventions of professional, middle-class people eager, "to seek legitimation for their own more conservative impulses."[27] In the early 1970s, ignoring rising labor militancy as well as racial, ethnic, and gender diversity among working-class people, the media effectively portrayed them as the new conservative bedrock of middle America. "All in the Family," the early 1970s television sitcom series that immortalized racist, chauvinist, working-class hero-buffoon Archie Bunker, can best be read, Ehrenreich suggests, as "the longest-running Polish joke," a projection of middle-class bad faith.[28] Yet, if this bad faith served professional middle-class interests, it did so at the expense of feminism. The inverse logic of class prejudice construed the constituency of that enormously popular social movement as exclusively middle-class. By convincing middle-class feminists of our isolation, perhaps the last laugh of that Polish joke was on us. Even Ehrenreich, who sensitively debunked the Bunker myth, labeled "startling" the findings of a 1986 Gallup poll that "56 percent of American women considered themselves to be 'feminists,' and the degree of feminist identification was, if anything, slightly higher as one descended the socioeconomic scale."[29] In order to transform the sentiments behind such poll data into effective political alliances, feminists need to transcend cardboard images of working-class and middle-class family values.

While my ethnographic research demonstrated the demise of *the* working-class family, in no way did it document the emergence of the classless society once anticipated by postindustrial theorists.[30] On the contrary, under postindustrial occupation and income distributions, the middle classes have been shrinking and the economic circumstances of Americans polarizing.[31] African-Americans have borne the most devastating impact of economic restructuring and the subsequent decline of industrial and unionized occupations.[32] But formerly privileged white working-class men, who achieved access to the American Dream in the 1960s and 1970s, like Pam's two husbands and Lou Lewison, came to find their gains threatened and nearly impossible to pass on to their children.[33]

While high-wage, blue-collar jobs declined, the window of postindustrial opportunity that once admitted men and women with limited educational backgrounds, like Lou and Kristina Lewison and Don Franklin, to middle-class status, also slammed shut. "During the 1980s, the educated got richer and the uneducated got poorer. And it looks like more of the same in the 1990s," declared a prophetic summary of occupational statistics from the Census Bureau and the Labor Department in 1989.[34] Young white families earned 20 percent less when I was conducting my fieldwork in 1986 than did comparable families in 1979, and their homeownership prospects plummeted.[35] Real earnings for young men between the ages of twenty and twenty-four had dropped by 26 percent between 1973 and 1986, while the military route to upward mobility that many of their fathers traveled constricted.[36] In the 1950s, men like Lou Lewison, equipped with VA loans, could buy homes with token downpayments and budget just 14 percent of their monthly wages for housing costs. By 1984, however, carrying a median-priced home would cost first-time, would-be homeowners 44 percent of an average male's monthly earnings.[37] Few could manage this, and in 1986 the U.S. government reported "the first sustained drop in home ownership since the modern collection of data began in 1940."[38]

Postindustrial shifts reduced blue-collar job opportunities for the under-educated sons of the working-class fathers I studied. And technological developments like Computer-Aided Design (CAD) escalated the entry criteria and reduced the ranks of those middle-level occupations which had only recently employed uncredentialed young people like Kristina Lewison and Pam's oldest child, Lanny.[39] The proportion of American families in the middle-income range fell from 46 percent in 1970 to 39 percent in 1985, and it has declined further since then. In the midst of the Reagan "recovery," two earners in a household had become necessary just to keep from losing ground.[40] Data like these led social analysts to anxiously track "the disappearing middle class," a phrase which, Barbara Ehrenreich aptly noted, "in some ways missed the point. It was the blue-collar working class that was 'disappearing,' at least from the middle range of comfort."[41]

Postindustrial restructuring had contradictory effects on the employment opportunities of former working-class women. Driven by declines in real family income, by desires for social achievement and independence, and by an awareness that committed male breadwinners were in increasingly scarce supply, such women flocked to expanding jobs in service, clerical, and new industrial occupations. Their jobs provided a new means of family subsidy or self-support as well as the self-respect gained by many women, like Pam and Dotty. Few, however, could enjoy earnings or prospects equivalent to those of their former husbands or fathers. Postindustrial economic restructuring replaced many white male workers with women and minority men, but in much lesser-paid, more vulnerable jobs.[42]

Whose Family Crisis?

This massive reordering of work, class and gender relationships during the past several decades turned family life into a contested terrain. It seems ironic, therefore, to observe that at the very time women were becoming the new proletariat, the postmodern family condition, even more than the modern family system that it was replacing, was proving to be a woman-tended domain. To be sure, as recent studies indicate, there is some empirical basis for the enlightened father imagery that Hollywood has been celebrating since the mid-1980s in films like *Kramer vs. Kramer* or the more recent Arnold Schwarzenegger comedy, *Junior*, and that has even become a prominent feature of Gary Trudeau's *Doonesbury* comic strip.[43] Indeed, my fieldwork corroborated emerging evidence that the determined efforts by feminists and many other working women to reintegrate men into family life have not been entirely without effect. There are data, for example, indicating that increasing numbers of men would sacrifice occupational gains in order to have more time with their families, just as there are data documenting actual increases in male involvement in child care.[44]

The excessive media attention that the faintest signs of new paternity enjoy, may, however, be a symptom of the deeper, far less comforting reality that it so effectively obscures. We have been experiencing, as Andrew Cherlin aptly puts it, "the feminization of kinship."[45] Demographers report a drastic decline in the average number of years that men live in households with young children.[46] Few of the women who assume responsibility for their children in 80 to 90 percent of divorce cases in the United States today had to wage a custody battle for this privilege.[47] We hear few proposals for a "daddy track." And few of the adults providing care to sick and elderly relatives are male.[48] Yet ironically, until recently, most of the alarmist, nostalgic literature about contemporary family decline attacked women, and especially feminists, for abandoning domesticity, the flipside of women's tardy entry into modernity. The anxious public outcries bemoaning destructive effects on families of working mothers, high divorce rates, institutionalized child care, or sexual liberalization rarely bothered to scrutinize the family behaviors of men. Rather, they generally blamed women, and particularly feminist women, for placing their personal and career interests ahead of those of their children and families. Particularly histrionic, but hardly unique, was the rhetoric in a promotional letter I received in 1990 for a new journal, *The Family in America*, which promised to cover such issues as "Vanishing Moms" and "Day Care: Thalidomide of the 90s."

Recently, however, politicians, journalists, and much of the public have become increasingly preoccupied with the problem of what David Blankenhorn terms "fatherlessness." The National Fatherhood Initiative which he directs, the Christian men's Promise Keepers movement, and the 1995 Million Man March of African-Americans all reflect this partial shift in public attention from the plight of motherless to that of fatherless children. I certainly welcome signs of awareness that, if there is a family crisis, it is primarily a male family crisis, just as I welcome serious efforts to encourage men to assume greater responsibility for children and family bonds. After all, the vast majority of women, like Pam and Dotty, have amply demonstrated a continuing commitment to sustaining kin ties. Unfortunately, however, too much of the new public concern with "fatherlessness" actually holds women and feminism largely responsible for men's absence from the lives of children. Women are now blamed for developing unreasonable familial expectations of men that frighten men away—particularly in regard to equal treatment and shared responsibility for children and housework. Women also are blamed for rejecting paternal participation in favor of rearing children on their own. Blankenhorn devotes a scornful chapter in *Fatherless America* to treating what he regards as emasculating, androgynous visions of "The New Father," that he attributes to feminists and their liberal cultural allies. "As a cultural proposition," Blankenhorn warns, "much of the New Father model depends upon denigrating or ignoring the historical meaning of fatherhood in America. Indeed, much of the New Father ideal is based explicitly upon belittling our own fathers."[49]

The historical meaning of fatherhood that Blankenhorn celebrates with the greatest nostalgia pays homage to the sort of 1950s suburban, breadwinner dads that Pam's first husband and Lou Lewison once had seemed to represent:

as a group, the fathers of the 1950s did rather well by their children, at least compared to the fathers who preceded and followed them. They got and stayed married. They earned a lot of money, much of which went to their children. . . . They spent more time with their children than their own fathers had with them, and also more than their sons, living in a divorce culture, would later spend with *their* children. They coached Little League, installed Sears swing sets in the backyard, took countless photos of the kids, attended games, practices, and school plays, puttered in the yard, took the garbage out, came home every night for dinner. They stayed around.

They were the most domesticated generation of fathers in modern American history.[50]

Thus, *in the name of The Father and of The Family*, Blankenhorn, Farrakhan, and a mounting crescendo of advocates of family values urge women to gratefully settle for a modified version of the modern family gender regime. In light of the increasingly difficult and dangerous familial conditions of the postindustrial, anti-welfare state regime, many women might readily agree with Pam that such a compromise would be, "not so bad a deal," were it genuinely available to them.

For most women, or men for that matter, even "such a deal" is beyond their reach. Nostalgia for the modern family order deflects public attention from the social sources of many of our most pervasive family troubles. Supply-side economics, governmental deregulation, and the right-wing assault on social welfare programs that began in the 1980s and has escalated in the 1990s have magnified the destabilizing effects of postindustrial occupational shifts not only on flagging modern families but also on emergent postmodern ones. Surveys suggest that providing financial security is the chief family concern reported by parents in the postindustrial United States.[51] Responding to economic and social insecurities at least as much as to feminism, higher percentages of families in almost all income groups have adopted a multiple-earner strategy.[52] Thus, the household form which has come closer than any other to replacing the modern family as a new cultural and statistical norm consists of a two-earner, heterosexual married couple with children.[53]

It is not likely, however, that any singular household type will soon achieve the measure of normalcy that the modern family long enjoyed. Indeed, the postmodern "success" of the voluntary principle of the modern family system precludes this, assuring a fluid, unstable familial culture. The routinization of divorce and remarriage generates a diversity of family patterns even greater than was characteristic of the premodern period when death prevented family stability or household homogeneity. Even cautious demographers judge the new family diversity to be, "an intrinsic feature . . . rather than a temporary aberration," of contemporary family life.[54]

In theory, the postmodern family condition of pluralism and flexibility should represent a democratic opportunity in which individuals' shared capacities, desires, and convictions could govern the character of their gender, sexual, and family relationships. Unfortunately, however, in this increasingly mean-spirited, practical world of contemporary economic retrenchment, political reaction, and social malaise, only a minority of primarily affluent citizens enjoy the kinds of resources that enable them to realize much of the tantalizing potential of postmodern family options. Little wonder that so many succumb to nostalgia for the modern family order. Yet we do not have the option of returning to that order, even if we truly wanted to. Instead, our urgent task is to begin to move forward, rather than backward, toward the postmodern family regime. We might do well to start distributing access to its opportunities, responsibilities, and hazards far more equitably, because for better and/or worse, the postmodern family revolution is here to stay.

CHAPTER 2

The Family Is Dead,
Long Live Our Families

.   .   .   .

THE UNITED NATIONS PROCLAIMED 1994 TO BE "THE INTERNATIONAL Year of The Family." However, *the family* is a peculiarly Western and modern concept. Some cultures do not employ the category "family" at all. Many societies that do use the term do so to depict diverse relationships and to convey diverse meanings. By the time the United Nations chose to commemorate the family, both the term and the kinship system it has come to signify had reached a state of intense transformation and political contest, particularly in the United States, but with reverberations worldwide. By proclaiming a global year of the family, the UN imposed deceptive unity on a contested term. Its use of the term also unwittingly derives from a declining theory of modernization that has been criticized as ethnocentric.

Modernization and The Family

In most of Europe and North America the family has become nearly synonymous with the nuclear household unit made up of a married, heterosexual couple and their biological or adopted children. Although popular usage more fluidly adapts the concept to refer to all people related through blood, marriage, or adoption, most Westerners do erroneously associate the family with nature and project it backward into a timeless past. However, historians have demonstrated that in the ancient world, the "Roman *familia* referred to all that which belonged to the *paterfamilias*, including slaves and servants, as well as relatives by blood or marriage."[1] Thus, the *Oxford English Dictionary* (O.E.D.) dates the first entry of the world "family" into the English language to just before the Renaissance, approximately in the year 1400, when it was used to indicate the servants of a house or household.[2] Historians estimate that during the fifteenth century, the vast majority of families (between two-thirds and three-fourths of all families) could not afford to rear their own children to adulthood.[3]

The *O.E.D.* places the contemporary popular meaning of family, "the group of persons consisting of the parents and their children, whether actually living together or not," as the *third* of eleven definitions it offers and places its earliest recorded usage in the late seventeenth century.[4] Only during the nineteenth century, in the Victorian era, did our present common meaning of family come to dominance. Until the mid-nineteenth century, historian John Gillis reminds us, "it was accepted that marriage was beyond the reach of many, and that most people would not grow up in the bosom of their families of origin."[5]

It is important to recognize, therefore, that the family is a product of those long historical transformations, generally referred to as modernization. Indeed, many historians employ the concept of the modern family, to describe the particular domestic arrangements which the family has come to designate. The modern family in the West developed historically out of a patriarchal, premodern family economy in which work and family life were thoroughly integrated. In the United States, the modern family system arose in the nineteenth century when industrialization turned men into breadwinners and women into homemakers by separating paid work from households. Beginning first among white, middle-class people, this family pattern came to represent modernity and success. Indeed the American way of life came to be so identified with this family form that the trade union movement struggled for nearly a century to secure for male workers the material condition upon which it was based—the male breadwinner wage. However, not until the mid-twentieth century did significant percentages of industrial workers achieve this access to the male breadwinner nuclear family, and it has always exceeded the reach of the vast majority of African-Americans. Slaves were not allowed to marry and had no parental rights at all, and few African-American households have ever been able to afford a full-time home-maker. In fact, many African-American mothers have worked as domestic workers in the modern-family homes of relatively privileged whites.[6]

The rise of the modern family system spelled the demise of the premodern, family economy which was explicitly patriarchal. Thus, it represented a shift in what sociologist Deniz Kanidyoti has called "patriarchal bargains."[7] In the classical patriarchal bargain, women accept overt subordination in exchange for protection and secure social status. The modern patriarchal bargain sugarcoats this exchange by wrapping it in an ideology of separate spheres and romantic love. In place of premodern marriages, which were arranged, in whole or in part, by parents and kin for economic, political, and social purposes, modern men and women, seeking love and companionship, voluntarily bind themselves for life to the complementary object of their individual desires. Under the guise of a separate but equal division of labor between male breadwinners and female homemakers, women and children became increasingly dependent upon the earnings of men. The nineteenth century gave rise to cults of "true womanhood," celebrating domesticity and maternalism. This generated conceptions of femininity that continue to infuse Western family ideology.[8] The development of analogous doctrines about the "tender years" of young children who need a specifically maternal form of love and care began to undermine earlier legal doctrines, which had treated children as patriarchal property.[9]

U.S. family patterns became more predictable and homogeneous as the modern family system evolved in the nineteenth and twentieth centuries. High mortality and remarriage rates had kept premodern family patterns diverse and complex, but declines in mortality enabled increasing numbers of people to anticipate a normal family life course. By the mid-twentieth century, modern family life patterns, from birth through courtship, marriage, work, childrearing, and death had become so homogeneous, normative, and predictable that the family began to appear natural, universal and self-evident.

Social scientists are rarely impervious to the tacit cultural understandings of their times. During the post–World War II period, family sociologists in the United States developed a theory of family modernization that was rooted in the conviction that U.S. family history would prove to be a global model. Arguing that the modern nuclear family was ideally suited to support the functioning of industrial society, and that it was both a product of and handmaiden to Enlightenment progress and democracy, social scientists predicted that it would spread throughout the modernizing world. A product of Western cultural imperialism, the family modernization thesis presumed that the superiority of Western cultural forms would insure their eventual triumph over the "backward" nations and peoples of the globe.[10] Indeed some family scholars came to argue that the early development of the modern nuclear family in the West facilitated the Western supremacy in developing capitalism.[11]

So convinced have Western governments been of the superiority of their family patterns that they have often imposed their gender and family patterns on conquered peoples. The United States, for example, disrupted matrilineal and extended kin systems among several indigenous New World cultures by awarding land titles exclusively to male-headed, nuclear household units.[12] In a similar fashion, Europeans have destructively imposed nuclear family principles on very different African kinship systems. In the Zambian copperbelt, for example, mineowners ignored and disrupted the actual extended kinship patterns of their workers by distributing benefits only to a worker's wife and children.[13] More often, however, Westerners presumed that the global diffusion of the modern nuclear family system would come about automatically. These rather contradictory ideas about the family—that it is natural and universal, on the one hand, and that it is a sign and agent of Western superiority, on the other—continue to collide in popular and scholarly discourse.

Contradictions of The Family

We can gain some perspective on contemporary family turmoil by recognizing contradictions inherent in the ideology, principles, and practices of the modern family system, the most glaring of which is the tension between volition and coercion. The ideology of the modern family construes marital commitment as a product of the free will and passions of two equal individuals who are drawn to each other by romantic attraction and complementary emotional needs. However, the domestic division of labor of the modern family system, which made women economically dependent upon male earners, and the subordination of women, both de jure and de facto, provided potent incentives for women to choose to enter and remain in marriages, quite apart from their individual desires. And while men certainly have always enjoyed greater opportunities to pursue their emotional and sexual interests inside and outside of marriage, until quite recently cultural codes and material sanctions led most men to depend upon the personal, emotional, and social services of a full-time homemaker. Political satirist Barbara Ehrenreich has observed that the white middle classes in the United States are likely the only bourgeoisie in history to employ members of their own class as personal servants.[14]

The relative acceptability of the contradiction between egalitarian principles of free love and companionship and inegalitarian forms of material and cultural coercion depended upon the availability and accessibility of a male breadwinner wage. Feminist historians have debated the degree to which working-class wives supported, resisted, or benefitted from the trade-union struggle that men conducted to earn wages sufficient to support fulltime homemakers and mothers.[15] However, no matter who achieved this arrangement, which Heidi Hartmann has called a patriarchal-capitalist bargain negotiated between male factory owners and laborers, it has proven to be quite ephemeral. The majority of industrial workers did not earn enough to support a full-time housewife until the 1950s or 1960s, and soon after they did so, deindustrialization and post-industrialization conspired to eliminate their jobs and erode their earnings.[16]

Thus, instability was written into the genetic code of the modern family system (on the "Y" chromosome), because its sustenance depended upon the wide availability of stable, liveable-wage jobs for men. As that strand of the bargain began to unravel during the 1970s and 1980s, the fragility of the entire gender and family order moved into full view, provoking widespread consternation over "family crisis" throughout advanced industrial societies.

During the past few decades, every developed industrial nation has experienced soaring divorce rates, falling birth rates, and rising rates of unmarried domestic partners, of step- and blended families, and of nonfamily households. Alarmists who decry family decline in the United States often overlook the transnational character of these demographic trends. A 1977 Viennese study warned that if the rate of increase in European divorce rates during the 1970s were to continue until the year 2000, at that point 85 percent of all European marriages would end in divorce.[17]

During this same period, the employment rates of women and men, formerly quite distinct, began to converge worldwide. Women, especially mothers of young children, now find it necessary to work for pay to support or contribute to the support of families that have been undermined by the loss of jobs and real earnings by men. The loss of steady work, or any work, for men at lower educational levels has been quite dramatic. While more than two-thirds of men with less than a high school education worked full time, year round during the 1970s, a decade later only half could find such steady work.[18] A significant wage gap between men and women persists, but the normalization of female employment and the decline in jobs for men has reduced some of women's economic dependency on men, and thus, has weakened one coercive buttress of marriage.

That is one major reason why single motherhood is rising around the globe, and why increasing percentages of single mothers have never been married. Sitcom heroine Murphy Brown has become a controversial symbol of the family circumstances of a small, but rising number of affluent, professional women in the U.S. who are choosing to become single mothers rather than to forego motherhood entirely. In reality, the vast majority of single-mother families confront dire economic circumstances.[19] At the same time that many women began choosing to become mothers alone, and for related reasons, birth rates were falling below replacement levels throughout the postindustrial world. It is particularly striking that women in Italy, an overwhelmingly Catholic country, now give birth to the smallest national average number of children in the advanced industrial world.[20] On the other hand, birth rates have begun to rise in Sweden, despite its reputation as the leading country for family decline.[21] The comparative level of security and confidence that prospective Swedish parents, particularly would-be mothers, derive from their nation's exceptionally progressive tax structure and social welfare provisions is the most likely explanation for this paradox. Meanwhile, the *New York Times* reports that "Eastern Germany's adults appear to have come as close to a temporary suspension of childbearing as any large population in the human experience," a response to the region's dire economic conditions since reunification. The state of Brandenburg has voted to offer parents a cash incentive of $650 per new child born.[22]

Because global capitalism is governed by the endless search for profits through increased productivity and technological development, we can be certain that our only social constant is change. Social change is a permanent and endless feature of our world, and all we can know about the future of family life is that it too will continue to change. Recent developments in reproductive technology and genetic engineering offer glimpses of some of the most dramatic and radical implications of future family scenarios. *Junior,* a 1994 Christmas season family movie starring Arnold Schwarzenegger as a pregnant experimental scientist, (a movie which proved to be more popular with women than men), presages some of the redefinitions of family life in store as science completes its Faustian gift of separating sexuality, conception, gestation, procreation, marriage, childrearing, and parenting. Pregnant men and test-tube babies, once the standard fare of science fiction, now appear inevitable. We have already reached the point at which a man's sperm can fertilize one woman's ovum, which gestates in the uterus of a second woman, who, in turn, serves as a "surrogate" for yet a third woman, who plans to adopt and rear the offspring, with or without a second man or a fourth woman as co-parent. What and who is the mother, the father, or the family in such a world?

The Postmodern Family Condition

The astonishing transformations sketched above indicate that the particular patriarchal bargain of the modern family system has collapsed. Instead, we now forge our intimate lives within the terms of the postmodern family condition described earlier. At the current moment in Western family history, no single family pattern is statistically dominant, and our domestic arrangements have become increasingly diverse. Only a minority of U.S. households still contain married couples with children; and many of these include divorced and remarried adults. More children live with single mothers than in modern families containing a breadwinner dad and a full-time homemaker mom.[23] Most features of the postmodern family condition are most prominent in the United States and Scandinavia. But demographic trends are similar throughout the highly industrialized world, with variations only in the degree, timing, and pace of the changes, but not in their direction. Once the family modernization thesis predicted that all the societies of the globe would converge toward a singular family system—the modern Western family system. Ironically, instead we are converging internationally toward the postmodern family condition of diversity, flux, and instability.

Under postmodern conditions, the social character of practices of gender, sexuality, parenting, and family life, which once appeared to be natural and immutable, become visible and politically charged. While similar demographic trends are dissolving the modern family system throughout the capitalist, industrialized world, national responses to the modern family crisis differ widely. Some societies have adapted to the decline of the male breadwinner family by devising generous social welfare policies that attempt to mitigate some of the destructive impact that marital fragility too often inflicts on children and the unequal burden it places on women. Again the Scandinavian countries, with Sweden and Norway in the lead, set the standards for innovative family support policies of this sort. In both nations, parents of either gender are entitled to apportion a full year's leave with 90 percent pay to take care of a newborn. Because so few fathers availed themselves of this benefit, both Sweden and Norway recently offered them added incentive to do so. Both countries now allow men, and only men, to receive an additional month of paid parental leave beyond the original twelve months, which men and women can allot as they choose. Moreover, Scandinavian workers enjoy paid leave to care for sick children and relatives, as well as universal family allowances, health care, including sex education, contraception, and abortion services, and subsidized high-quality daycare. There are few deadbeat dads in these Nordic nations, because the state assumes responsibility for collecting and distributing child care payments. As a result, while more than half of single-parent families in the United States live below the official poverty line, in Sweden only 2 percent do so.[24] Most likely this is why Swedish women have been willing to bear more children in recent years. Likewise, Sweden and Norway also followed Denmark's lead in legalizing a form of marriage for same-sex couples before this became a visible political issue in the United States.[25]

Other affluent societies, however, have proven far more hostile to postmodern demographic and cultural changes. They are far less willing to assume public responsibility for addressing the unjust and disruptive effects caused by these changes. The United States is far and away the most extreme in this regard. Reflecting an exceptionally privatized economy, an individualistic culture, and racial antagonisms, social welfare for the poor in the United States has always been comparatively stingy, punitive, and unpopular. Yet even this meager system is currently being dismantled. The United States alone, among 18 advanced industrial nations, does not provide its citizens with universal health coverage, family allowances, or paid parental leaves.[26] In fact, it was not until the Family Leave Act of 1993 that the right to take an unpaid three-month maternity leave, which few families can afford to use, was mandated for workers in firms with at least 50 employees. Welfare provisions in the United States have always been means-tested, stigmatized, and niggardly.[27] As a result, a higher percentage of single-mother families in the United States as well as a higher percentage of children in general, live in poverty than in any advanced industrial nation.[28] Conservative estimates of the numbers that current welfare reform legislation will add to this disturbing record have even frightened Senator Moynihan, one of the original advocates of revising the welfare system.[29]

While family support policies in the United States are the weakest in the industrial world, no society has yet to come close to our expenditure of politicized rhetoric over family crisis. The politics of gender, sexuality, reproduction, and family here are the most polarized, militant, and socially divisive in the world, precisely because social structural responses to the decline of the modern family system have been so weak. This is an important reason why feminism, gay liberation, and backlash "profamily" movements are so vocal and influential across the political spectrum.

Rampant nostalgia for the modern family system, or more precisely, for an idealized version of a 1950s Ozzie and Harriet image of the family, has become an increasingly potent ideological force in the United States, with milder versions evident in Canada and England.[30] Fundamentalist Christians and right-wing Republicans spearheaded the profamily movement that abetted the Reagan "revolution" of the 1980s. By the 1994 electoral season, however, even President Clinton had embraced the ideology of an explicitly centrist campaign for family values led by a small group of social scientists. This ongoing campaign portrays family breakdown as the primary source of social malaise in the United States, blaming the decline of the married-couple family for everything from crime, violence, and declining educational standards to poverty, drug abuse, and sexually transmitted disease.[31]

There seems to be nearly an inverse relationship between a nation's rhetorical concern over the plight of children in declining families and its willingness to implement policies to ease their suffering. This may appear paradoxical, if not hypocritical, but family support policies are consistent with the historical development of public responsibility for social welfare in each nation. They are strongest in parliamentary governments in which labor movements have achieved a significant voice.[32] Lip service to the family, on the other hand, serves as a proxy for the private sphere and as a rationale for abdicating public responsibility for social welfare. Unfortunately, the more individualistic and market-oriented a society becomes, the more difficult it becomes to sustain family bonds.

Let's Bury "the Family"

The decision of the United Nations to proclaim an "International Year of The Family" represents a tacit acknowledgment that family systems are in crisis around the world. This choice of language, however, proclaims an oxymoronic project, because it begs the question of a universally shared definition of the family. Indeed, the UN Committee on the Family that was responsible for organizing the

family year recognized, but tried to evade, this dilem
prefaced its official set of guiding principles on the family with the
claim that "no definition of the family is given because of the great
variety of types, cultures, and customs existing in families throughout
the world. . . ." Yet, it also issued a report entitled "Family in Crisis,"
which began by acknowledging that, "to identify crises which beset
families today is not feasible without clarifying what we mean by
family." Finally, the same document concluded with the astonishing
admission that, "we are aware that the family does not exist."[33]

The family indeed is dead, if what we mean by it is the modern
family *system* in which units comprised of male breadwinner and
female homemaker, married couples, and their offspring dominate
the land. But its ghost, the ideology of the family, survives to haunt
the consciousness of all those who refuse to confront it. It is time to
perform a social autopsy on the corpse of the modern family system
so that we may try to lay its troublesome spirit to rest. Perhaps, a
proper memorial service for the family system we have lost can free
us to address the diverse needs of people struggling to sustain intimate relationships under very difficult postmodern family conditions.

Adopting the pathologist's stance of hard-hearted, clinical de-
tachment in this case can lead to an uncomfortable conclusion.
Historically, all stable systems of marriage and family life have rested
upon diverse measures of coercion and inequality. Family *systems*
appear to have been most stable when women and men have been
economically interdependent, when households served as units of
production with sufficient resources to reproduce themselves, and
when individuals lacked alternative means of economic, sexual, and
social life. Family units of this sort have always been embedded in,
supported, and sanctioned by wider sets of kinship, community, and
religious ties. Disturbingly, all such family systems have been patriarchal. The stability of the modern family system, which represented
a significant departure from several of these principles, depended
upon the adequacy and reliability of the male family wage. However,

the ceaseless development of capitalist industrialization, which disrupted the premodern patriarchal bargain, has now disrupted the modern one as well, and it will continue to disrupt postmodern familial regimes of any sort.

It is sobering to recognize that throughout history, family crises have been resolved by replacing one male-dominant form of domestic life with another. The Chinese revolution, for example, supplanted Confucian patriarchy with patriarchal-socialism.[34] In the West, The Family resolved the crisis industrialization had induced in the premodern family economy. The modern family system offered women both gains and losses over the prior patriarchal bargain, but now it too has outlived its historic role.

Patriarchal crises are always moments of intense danger and opportunity. Under postmodern family conditions throughout the postindustrial world, women enjoy greater access to education and employment, and a greater need for both, than ever before. As women become less dependent upon male earnings, they are freer to leave or avoid abusive or hostile relationships. At the same time, however, men seem to feel less obliged to commit themselves to familial or parental responsibilities, and more and more women confront the added burdens of the double day. In Eastern Europe, on the other hand, the collapse of the communist patriarchal bargain has unleashed a different kind of patriarchal crisis. Although many women have been freed from mandatory second shifts and ration queues, many have also lost their access to employment, abortion, and child care, not to speak of food and life itself. Little wonder that as women struggle to survive diverse patriarchal crises, they too can become nostalgic for the relative security provided by prior, more stable, patriarchal forms.

The Family of Woman

During the late 1950s, just when the modern family system was about to unravel, a humanist book of photographs, *The Family of Man*, enjoyed immense popularity in the U.S.[35] The postmodern family condition that has emerged since then could more aptly be called "the family of woman." Public discourse is preoccupied with the growing ranks of single mothers and fatherless children. The frequently noted feminization of poverty around the globe is a direct product of the feminization of family life that has been taking place since the collapse of the modern industrial order upon which the modern family system depended.

Under conditions of postindustrial, global capitalism, marital instability and woman-centered kin ties are becoming endemic facts of life. This presents postindustrial societies with only two real, and imperfect, options. A nation can choose to recognize and adapt to the new realities, however unwelcome, by assuming greater social responsibility for the welfare of children and citizens, as Scandinavian societies have tried to do; or, societies can resist, deny, and rail against the facts of postmodern family life, resorting to the rhetoric of moral panic and the politics of backlash, so popular in the United States.

Perhaps the postmodern "family of woman" will take the lead in burying The Family at long last. The Family is a concept derived from faulty theoretical premises and an imperialist logic, which even at its height never served the best interests of women, their children, or even of many men. We should not be misled by its false gender neutrality. The International Year of The Family was a year like most years, when women often suffered the brunt of family crises and struggled, against increasingly difficult odds, to sustain their kin and spirits. Women, in particular, should be resisting the forces of denial and the backlash against family change. Attacks against welfare are attacks on mothers struggling to sustain vulnerable families. To resist the campaign for family values is by no means to be anti-family. Instead, women should lead efforts to expand public support for an expanded definition of family, one that is honest and tolerant enough to acknowledge and support the diversity of family patterns, preferences, and relationships in which we actually live. It is time to lay to rest the ghost of The Family so that we may begin to build a safe world for living families. The family is dead. Long live our families!

CHAPTER 3

The Neo-Family-Values
Campaign

. . . .

IN NOVEMBER OF 1992 THERE WAS IMPECCABLE CAUSE TO IMAGINE
that family wars in the United States were about to abate. The extent
and irreversibility of family change, assisted by Murphy Brown, the
Republican Convention fiasco and the Year of the Woman, seemed
to have vanquished the family-values brigades, while "the economy,
stupid" had lured many Reagan Democrats back from their fling
with supply-side economics. Who would have predicted that even
the liberal media would scramble to rehabilitate Dan Quayle's image
before Bill and Hillary had survived their blistering first 100 days?

Yet that is exactly what happened. DAN QUAYLE WAS RIGHT, blared
the April 1993 cover of the *Atlantic* monthly, a magazine popular
with the very cultural elite whom the former vice president had
blamed for the decline of Western civilized family life. Far from
withering, a revisionist campaign for family values flourished under
Democratic skies. While Clinton's job stimulus package suffered a
silent demise, pro-family-values stories mushroomed in magazines,
newspapers, on radio and TV talk shows, and in scholarly journals.
The *Atlantic* cover story by Barbara Dafoe Whitehead[1] ignited "the

52 . . .

single strongest public response to any issue ever published by the *Atlantic* since at least 1981,"[2] and was recycled from sea to rocky sea. A *New York Times* op-ed, "The Controversial Truth: Two-Parent Families are Better," by Rutgers University sociologist David Popenoe, also enjoyed acclaim, with retreads and derivatives appearing from the *Chronicle of Higher Education* to the Santa Rosa, California *Press Democrat*.[3] In the winter of 1992–1993 issue of *American Scholar*, Senator Daniel Patrick Moynihan, a founding father of post–World War II family crisis discourse, added to his hefty inventory of family values jeremiads. James Q. Wilson, the Collins Professor of Management and Public Policy at UCLA, earlier proponent of racial theories of criminality, weighed in with a featured family-values essay in *Commentary*.[4] From "This Week with David Brinkley" to the "MacNeil-Lehrer News Hour," television followed suit, featuring guests like Popenoe, who chanted kaddish over an idealized family past.

Less a revival than a creative remodel job, the 1990s media blitz on family values signals the considerable success of a distinctively new political phenomenon. Because the rhetoric of family–values discourse seems so familiar, most progressives have failed to recognize, or to respond appropriately to, what is dangerously novel here. I would have committed a similar error, had my book, *Brave New Families*, not become a target for the new, family security guards.[5] Quoting from it, Popenoe portrayed me as an anti-family extremist, and numerous spin-offs reprinted the lines while deriding my support for family diversity.[6] This unsolicited notoriety fueled my efforts to understand how and why a revival of the family-values campaign coincided with the very changing of the political guard that I had expected would spell its decline.

Pseudo-Scholarly Cultural Combat

Old-fashioned family-values warriors, like Jerry Falwell, Dan Quayle, and Pat Buchanan, are right-wing Republicans and/or fundamentalist Christians, overtly anti-feminist, anti-homosexual and politically reactionary. Their profamily campaign, which provided zeal and zeitgeist for both of Reagan's victories, enjoyed its heyday in the 1980s and suffered its nadir during the 1992 electoral season—from Quayle's infamous Murphy Brown speech through the ill-advised family-values orgy of the Republican Convention, and to defeat at the polls. This campaign continues to exert powerful influence over the Republican Party. In contrast, the revisionist campaign has an explicitly centrist politics, rhetoric, and ideology. A product of academicians rather than clerics, it grounds its claims in secular social science instead of religious authority, and eschews anti-feminism for a post-feminist family ethic.

While the right wing may prove the prime beneficiary of current family-values discourse, it is not its primary producer. Rather, an interlocking network of scholarly and policy institutes, think tanks, and commissions began mobilizing during the late 1980s to forge a national consensus on family values that rapidly shaped the family ideology and politics of the Clinton administration and his New Democratic party. Central to this effort are the Institute for American Values, co-directed by David Blankenhorn and Barbara Dafoe Whitehead (author of the *Atlantic* article), and its sponsored research offshoot, the Council on Families in America, co-chaired by David Popenoe and Jean Bethke Elshtain. The former, which Popenoe describes as a "nonpartisan public policy organization," sponsors the latter, whose seventeen members depict themselves as "a volunteer, nonpartisan program of scholarly research and interdisciplinary deliberation on the state of families in America. We come from across the human sciences and across the political spectrum."[7]

"This is an attempt to bring people together who could convince the liberal intelligentsia that the family was in trouble and that this was a big problem," Popenoe explained to me in an interview. "Most of us are neoliberal—you know, New Democrats, affiliated with the Progressive Policy Institute. We try to keep to the middle of the road."[8] The political networks and the funding sources of these center-laners merge with those of the communitarians—a movement characterized by its founder, sociologist Amitai Etzioni, as "strug-gling for the soul of the Clinton Administration."[9] They are linked as well with those of the Democratic Leadership Council's Progressive Policy Institute. Political scientist William Galston, who was Clinton's chief domestic policy adviser until he resigned in June of 1995, is a communitarian as well as a member of the Council on Families. Blankenhorn, Popenoe and Elshtain are all communitar-ians, as is Henry Cisneros. Al Gore spoke at a 1991 communitarian teach-in.

Galston co-authored a family policy position paper for the Pro-gressive Policy Institute,[10] which echoed themes from a conference co-sponsored by the Institute for American Values at Stanford Uni-versity in 1990. The conference volume, *Rebuilding the Nest*, edited by Blankenhorn, Elshtain, and Steven Bayme, helped guide the deliberations of the National Commission on Children, which is-sued the 1991 Rockefeller Report, *Beyond Rhetoric: A New American Agenda for Children and Families*.[11] Governor Bill Clinton of Ar-kansas was a member of that commission.

According to Popenoe these groups share the same benefactors, like the Randall, Smith Richardson, Scaife, and Mott foundations, and the Brookings and American Enterprise institutes; more of them are conservative than liberal as Popenoe acknowledged.[12] With such support, revisionists are self-consciously waging a cultural crusade, one modeled explicitly on the anti-smoking campaign, to restore the privileged status of lifelong, heterosexual marriage. Declaring that "the principal source of family decline over the past three decades has been cultural," Whitehead urged the Institute for American Val-ues readership to join a cultural mobilization to restore nuclear family supremacy.[13] Wilson's *Commentary* essay went further, call-ing "this raging cultural war" over family values, "far more conse-quential than any of the other cleavages that divide us."[14] *Newsweek* columnist Joe Klein applauded revisionist proposals for "a massive anti-pregnancy [sic] and proselytizing campaign similar to the anti-smoking and -drug crusades of recent years. 'Those *worked*,' says presidential adviser William Galston. 'They really changed behavior patterns, and this might, too.' "[15] Likewise, when Blankenhorn addressed a corporate-sponsored, invitational public forum on crime that I attended in San Francisco in the fall of 1995, he made the remarkable claim that, "there is one main thing going on out there in this country—the absence of fathers," and that in order to address it, "the most important thing to change is our minds."[16]

If the effects of this campaign on sexual and conjugal behaviors in the private sphere remain to be seen, it quickly achieved an astonishing, and disturbing, impact on the public behavior and policy priorities of the Clinton administration. It took scarcely a year to convert Clinton from representing himself as a proud icon of a strong single mom's glory into a repentant Quayle acolyte. "Hurray for Bill Clinton. What a different a year makes," Quayle gloated in December 1993, right after *Newsweek* had published the president's revised family credo: "Remember the Dan Quayle speech? There were a lot of very good things in that speech," Clinton acknowledged. "Would we be a better-off society if babies were born to married couples? You bet we would."[17] The rhetorical means through which Clinton's family-values makeover occurred merit close scrutiny.

Feigning Iconoclastic Courage

In one of the more effective rhetorical ploys of the revisionist campaign, these mainstream social scientists, policy lobbyists, and prominent political officeholders and advisers have been able to ride the coattails of the anti-political correctness crusade by positioning themselves as dissident challengers of a formidable, intolerant, ideological establishment. Popenoe, for example, is associate dean of Social and Behavioral Sciences at Rutgers University, as well as co-director of the Council on Families in America. Wilson occupies an endowed professorship of management and public policy at UCLA, and Elshtain, an endowed professorship of theology at the University of Chicago. Etzioni was the 1994–1995 President of the American Sociological Association. And Senator Moynihan, well. . . .

Yet, Wilson characterizes those scholars who reject a nostalgic view of 1950s families, as "policy elites."[18] During a radio debate over the superiority of the two-parent family, Popenoe portrayed me and other feminist sociologists as part of the "liberal social science establishment."[19] Whitehead laments, "it is nearly impossible to discuss changes in family structure without provoking angry protest,"[20] citing as evidence enraged responses in the mid-1960s to Moynihan's *The Negro Family: The Case for National Action*, which had labeled the rising percentages of Black single-mother families a "tangle of pathology." She attributes to ideological pressures some of the caution exercised by researchers who do not support the claim that single-parent families are deficient. "Some are fearful that they will be attacked by feminist colleagues," Whitehead claims, "or, more generally, that their comments will be regarded as an effort to turn back the clock to the 1950s—a goal that has almost no constituency in the academy."[21]

Wilson predicted that were the President to exercise leadership in condemning unwed childbearing, he would elicit "dismayed groans from sitcom producers and ideological accusations from sociology professors [like yours truly], but at least the people would know that he is on their side."[22] Exploiting popular resentment against PC, cultural elites builds upon the tradition of disingenuous populism honed by former Republican vice-presidents Spiro Agnew and Dan Quayle. At the same time, it pays tribute to the considerable, albeit precarious, influence over gender and family discourse that feminism has achieved during the past quarter-century. Inside the academy, many centrists probably do feel threatened and displaced by feminist scholars. They are fighting back.

Constructing Social Scientific Stigma

While the right-wing family-values campaign appeals to religious and traditional patriarchal authority for its family vision, centrists are engaged in an active process of transmuting into a newly established, social scientific "truth," one of the most widely held prejudices about family life in North America—the belief in the superiority of families composed of married, heterosexual couples and their biological children. Revisionists argue that the presence or absence of two married, biological parents in the household is the central determinant of a child's welfare, and thereby of our society's welfare. They identify fatherless families as the malignant root of escalating violence and social decay, claiming such families generate the lineage of unemployed, undomesticated, family-less fathers, as John Gillis aptly puts it,[23] who threaten middle-class tranquility.

Through the sheer force of categorical assertion, repetition, and cross-citation of each other's publications, these social scientists seem to have convinced most of the media, the literate public, and Clinton himself that a fault-free bedrock of social science research validates the particular family values that they and most Americans claim to favor, but fail to practice. "In three decades of work as a social scientist," asserted Popenoe in his *New York Times* op-ed, "I know of few other bodies of data in which the weight of evidence is so decisively on one side of the issue: on the whole for children, two-parent families are preferable to single-parent and stepfamilies."[24] In the *Atlantic* story three months later, Whitehead quoted these very lines as authority for a similar assertion: "The social arrangement that has proved most successful in ensuring the physical survival and promoting the social development of the child is the family unit of the biological mother and father."[25] Whitehead also relied on Moynihan's essay "Defining Deviancy Down," which blamed "broken families" for almost all of our current social crises. Moynihan, in turn, had quoted an earlier essay by Whitehead in support of a similar argument.[26] Moynihan, Whitehead, and Popenoe all cited the National Commission on Children's Rockefeller Report, and the Report returned the favor with frequent citations to essays by Popenoe and his associates in the Institute for American Values and the Council for Families in America.[27]

Then, when in April 1993 Popenoe defined the ideal family in the *Chronicle of Higher Education,*" he paraphrased views that he and Blankenhorn both had expressed in *Rebuilding the Nest* and which Whitehead and the Rockefeller Report had endorsed: "What are the characteristics of an *ideal* family environment for childrearing? The Council believes they are an enduring family with two biological parents that regularly engages in activities together; has many of its own routines, traditions, and stories; and provides a great deal of contact between adults and children."[28] With minor editorial revisions, the Council on Families in America reprinted this definition as one of eight propositions on family life.[29]

It is not often that the social construction, or more precisely here, the political construction of knowledge is quite so visible or incestuous as in the reciprocal citation practices of these cultural crusaders. Through such means they seem to have convinced President Clinton and most of the public that "it is a confirmed empirical generalization," as Popenoe maintains, that nontraditional families, "are not as successful as conventional two-parent families."[30] Yet, the current status of social scientific knowledge of the success of diverse family structures is far more complex, and the views of family scholars far more heterogeneous, than revisionists pretend. Social scientists continue actively to debate whether family form or processes determine diverse family outcomes and whether our family or socioeconomic crisis has generated its counterpart.[31] For example, in a judicious, comprehensive review essay on the cumulative research on changing parent-child relations, prominent family sociologist, David Demo, concluded that, "the consequences of maternal employment, divorce, and single-parent family structure have been greatly exaggerated, and that researchers need to investigate processes more directly influencing children, notably economic hardship and high levels of marital and family conflict."[32] In fact, according to Demo, "the accumulated evidence is sufficiently consistent to wonder whether we, as researchers, are asking the most important questions, or whether we, like the families we are trying to study, are more strongly influenced by traditional notions of family formality."[33]

The revisionist social scientists suppress these debates by employing social-scientific sleights-of-hand. For example, they rest their claims on misleading comparison groups and on studies, like Judith Wallerstein's widely cited research on divorcing parents, that do not use any comparison groups at all.[34] While it is true that, on average, children whose parents divorce fare slightly worse than those whose parents remain married, this reveals little about the impact of divorce on children. To address that question, one must compare children of divorce not with all children of married parents, but with those whose unhappily married parents do not divorce. In fact, research indicates that high-conflict marriages harm children more than do low-conflict divorces. "There is abundant evidence," David Demo concludes, "that levels of family conflict are more important than type of family structure for understanding children's adjustment, self-esteem, and other measures of psychological well-being."[35] Unhappily married parents must ask themselves not whether divorcing or staying married is worse for children in general, but which would be worse for their particular children in their particular unhappy marriage.

Centrists use additional statistical tricks to exaggerate advantages some children from two-parent families enjoy over their single-parented peers. For example, they pretend that correlation proves causality and ignore mediating variables, or they treat small and relative differences as though they were gross and absolute. In fact, most children from both kinds of families turn out reasonably all right, and when other parental resources—like income, education, self-esteem and a supportive, social environment—are roughly similar, signs of two-parent privilege largely disappear. Most research indicates that a stable, intimate relationship with one responsible, nurturant adult is a child's surest route to becoming the same kind of adult. In short, the research scale tips handily toward those who stress the quality of family relationships over their form.[36]

Once dissenting scholarly views on the pathology of single-parent families had been muffled or marginalized, only a rhetorical baby step was needed to move from the social to the moral inferiority of such families. Ergo, the remarkably respectful public response that

American Enterprise Institute scholar Charles Murray received in November 1993 to his overtly punitive quest to restigmatize unwed childbearing via Dickensian welfare policies. "My proposition is that illegitimacy is the single most important social problem of our time — more important than crime, drugs, poverty, illiteracy, welfare, or homelessness because it drives everything else," Murray declared in defense of his proposal, "to end all economic support for single mothers." Forcing single mothers off of welfare would slash nonmarital childbearing, Murray reasoned, because, "the pressure on relatives and communities to pay for the folly of their children will make an illegitimate birth the socially horrific act it used to be, and getting a girl pregnant something boys do at the risk of facing a shotgun."[37] Instead of receiving timely visits from the ghosts of Christmases past, present, and future, Murray was soon the featured guest on "This Week with David Brinkley." Even in liberal San Francisco, an op-ed by a supporter of Murray's proposals from the right-wing Hoover Institute upstaged the more charitable Christmas week commentaries aired on the local affiliate of National Public Radio.[38]

By then, revisionists had deftly paved the yellow brick road to Murray's media coronation. "Bringing a child into the world outside of marriage," Blankenhorn had asserted three years earlier, "is almost always personally and socially harmful."[39] In December of 1992, Moynihan congratulated himself on having predicted the epidemic of single-parent families and its calamitous social consequences nearly 30 years earlier. "There is one unmistakable lesson in American history," he had written in 1965; "a community that allows a large number of young men to group up in broken families, dominated by women . . . asks for and gets chaos."[40] In April 1993, just as Whitehead's *Atlantic* essay hit the stands, Wilson explicitly advised President Clinton that, to honor his populist pretensions, he should "say that it is wrong—not just imprudent, but wrong—to bear children out of wedlock."[41]

Thus, by the time the 1993 holiday season began, the ideological mortar had dried firmly enough to encourage *Newsweek* columnist Joe Klein's view that "the issue is so elemental, the question so basic, the answer so obvious," that one should not have to ask a president, as the magazine just had done, whether it is "immoral for people to have children out of wedlock?" Klein applauded when President Clinton, himself possessed of dubious parentage and out-of-wedlock, half-siblings who seem to surface intermittently, answered, "much as Dan Quayle, to whom he gave considerable credit, might have: 'I believe this country would be a lot better off if children were born to married couples.'" After all, Klein lamented:

> It's a measure of our social fragility and moral perversity that the president's statement will be controversial in certain circles even though there's now a mountain of data showing illegitimacy to be the smoking gun in a sickening array of pathologies — crime, drug abuse, physical and mental illness, welfare dependency. Bill Clinton's morality will, no doubt, be seen as hopelessly retro — or worse, as cynical politics — in Hollywood, where he was off raising money over the weekend and where out-of-wedlock births are quite the fashion.[42]

Indeed, by then, the revisionist cultural onslaught had been so effective that even Donna Shalala, the token feminist progressive in Clinton's cabinet, felt politically compelled to recite its moralist mantra: "I don't like to put this in moral terms, but I do believe that having children out of wedlock is just wrong." A dyed-in-the-wool, but curious, White House liberal confided, off the record, to *Newsweek*, "I'd like to see the Murray solution tried somewhere — just to see, y'know, what might happen."[43] In June 1994, *before* the right-wing Republican mid-term electoral rout, Clinton sent a welfare reform proposal to Congress with caps on childbearing and benefits that threaten to satisfy such curiosity.

The New Postfeminist Familism

Despite inflated claims to iconoclasm, revisionists promote family values that seem, at first glance, tediously familiar. Sounding like card-carrying conservatives in academic drag, they blame family breakdown for everything from child poverty, declining educational standards, substance abuse, homicide rates, AIDS, infertility, and teen pregnancy to narcissism and the Los Angeles riots. They attribute family breakdown, in turn, to a generalized decline in family values, which, in its turn, they often associate with feminism, the sexual revolution, gay liberation, excessively generous welfare policies and escalating demands for social rights.

While orthodox and revisionist family preachers share obvious affinities, centrists take wiser note of present demographic and cultural terrain than do their right-wing counterparts. Because they claim to decry rampant individualism, they tend to acknowledge greater public and corporate responsibility for family decline and redress than is palatable to family values hardliners. Many used to claim to support the Progressive Policy Institute's call for a guaranteed working wage that would lift families with full-time workers out of poverty. Most also claim to favor family-friendly workplace reforms like flextime, family leaves, and flexible career paths.[44] Disappointingly, however, they devote much less of their political energies to these more progressive goals than to the cultural campaign which has done much to undermine such reforms.

Perhaps the most significant distinction between the traditional and neo-family values campaigns is in gender ideology. Departing from the explicit anti-feminism and homophobia of a Jesse Helms or Pat Buchanan, family centrists accommodate their family values to postindustrial society and postfeminist culture.[45] They temper their palpable nostalgia for Ozzie and Harriet with rhetorical gestures toward gender equality. "The council does not bemoan the loss of 'the traditional nuclear family,' with its strict social roles, distinguishing between male breadwinners and female homemakers," Popenoe maintains. "Recognizing," instead "the importance of female equality and the changing conditions of modern society, we do not see the previous model of lifelong, separate gender roles within marriage as either desirable or possible on a society-wide scale. But we do believe strongly that the model of the two-parent family, based on a lasting,

monogamous marriage, is both possible and desirable."[46] Blankenhorn too has espoused postfeminist ideology: "strengthening family
life in the 1990s cannot and should not mean the repeal of the past
30 years of new opportunities for women in the workplace and in
public life. Just as today's cultural ethos of individualism affects men
just as much as women, so must a revived ethos of family life affect
the behavior and priorities of both sexes."[47]

Revisionists place great emphasis on reviving paternal commitment. Wilson lauds efforts by the National Center for Neighborhood
Enterprise "that try to encourage men to take responsibility for their
children."[48] Whitehead praises a high-powered Boston attorney who
"left his partnership at a law firm and took a judgeship that gave him
more manageable hours," so that he could spend more time with his
children and his wife, also an attorney, who left trial law for more
family-friendly work.[49] Similarly, Galston cited his paternal priorities
when he resigned as White House domestic-policy adviser to return
to his university professorship in June 1995: "I told the president,
'You can replace me and my son can't.' "[50]

Blankenhorn has turned combatting fatherlessness into his over-
arching mission. Joining forces with Don Eberly, a former aide to
Jack Kemp, he formed a national organization of fathers to "restore
to fatherhood a sense of pride, duty, and reward."[51] Combining a
massive promotional tour for his 1995 book, *Fatherless America*, with
a campaign for The National Fatherhood Initiative, Blankenhorn
has been actively crusading against "excesses of feminism" like the
belief that "men will not become new fathers unless they do half the
diaper changes or bottle feedings." Instead, his campaign promotes a
neo-traditional model of fatherhood, in which, "the old father, with
some updating in the nurturing department, will do just fine."[52]

Such postfeminist ideology appeals to many conservative feminists and to many liberals. It builds upon a body of thought I once
labeled new conservative feminism, to which family centrists Elshtain and Sylvia Hewlett made formative contributions.[53] One of the
defining features of this ideology is its weak stomach for sexual pol-

itics. Centrists offer tepid support, at best, for abortion rights, often supporting restrictions like spousal and parental notification, partly with the claim that these could hold men more paternally accountable.[54] And as communitarian founder Etzioni put it, "there are some issues, such as abortion and gay rights, that we know communitarians cannot agree on, so we have completely avoided them."[55]

Rather than confront the internal contradictions, unjust power relations, and economic reorganization which underlie the decline of lifelong marriage, revisionists promote what Whitehead terms a New Familism, in which postfeminist women willingly, admirably, and self-consciously *choose* to place familial needs above the demands of "a life defined by traditional male models of career and success." "In the period of the New Familism," Whitehead exults, "both parents give up something in their work lives in order to foster their family lives. The woman makes the larger concession, but it is one she actively elects and clearly sees as temporary."[56] Popenoe explicitly proposes what he calls "revising the cultural script," for modern marriages by making such "temporary," asymmetrical gender concessions a normative feature in his model of the "modified traditional nuclear family."[57] Blankenhorn's bioevolutionary view of parenthood goes much further than Whitehead or Popenoe in its scorn for feminist and androgynous family values. "Ultimately, the division of parental labor is the consequence of our biological embodiment as sexual beings and of the inherent requirements of effective parenthood." His vision of rehabilitated paternity embraces only slightly modified forms of traditional paternal authority and responsibility:

> Historically, the good father protects his family, provides for its material needs, devotes himself to the education of his children, and represents his family's interests in the larger world. This work is necessarily rooted in a repertoire of inherited male values. . . . These values are not limited to toughness, competition, instrumentalism, and aggression—but they certainly include them. These "hard" male values have changed

and will continue to change. But they will not disappear or turn into their opposites. Nor should we wish them to.[58]

. . . And Other Euphemisms for Injustice:

1. **The "Stability" of Gender Inequality**   One need hardly be a paranoid feminist to penetrate the shallow veneer of revisionist commitments to gender equality. Defending a lengthy lament by Popenoe about American family decline, family sociologist Norval Glenn, for example, conceded that there is "a rational basis for concern that attempts to 'put the family back together' may tend to erase recent feminist gains." Likewise, Wilson acknowledged that, "what is at stake, of course, is the role of women."[59]

Of course. Few feminists were confused when Quayle lashed out at Murphy Brown. Perhaps a few more will be misled by the higher-toned, centrist retread of his views. Yet, despite lip-service to gender equality, the revisionist campaign does not redress marital inequalities or question that women bear disproportionate responsibility for their children and families. Rather, in the guise of rejecting "male models," it adds to the unjust burden of guilt, anxiety and marginality that divorced, unmarried, and unhappily married mothers already suffer. That Wilson and Glenn recognize the gender stakes in this rhetorical contest underscores how much more communitarian talk of family values impugns the individualism of women than that of men. Postfeminist familist ideology appropriates some feminist critiques of conventionally masculine work priorities while appealing to those conventionally feminine maternalist values of women that some feminist scholars like Carol Gilligan and Deborah Tannen have made popular. This ideology also exploits women's weariness with the incompatibility of postindustrial work and family demands, as well as their anxiety over the asymmetrical terms of the heterosexual courtship and marriage market and of women's vulnerability to divorce-induced poverty.

Centrists often blame excessive divorce rates as well as unwed motherhood on a general rise of selfishness—gender unspecified. To curb such indulgence they advocate measures to restrict access to divorce, such as mandatory waiting periods and counseling and the reinstatement of fault criteria in divorce laws. Typically they present their proposals for these restrictive measures under a child-centered mantle that taps women's all-too-ready reservoirs of guilt about failing to serve the best interests of their children. For example, Hillary Clinton prefaces her support for mandatory "cooling off" periods and counseling for parents considering divorce with the explanation that: "with divorce as easy as it is, and its consequences so hard, people with children need to ask themselves whether they have given a marriage their best shot and what more they can do to make it work before they call it quits."[60]

The backlash against no-fault divorce is gaining popularity among politicians. Republican Governor Terry Brandstad of Iowa denounced no-fault divorce in his 1996 State of the State Message. In February 1996, Michigan became the first state to consider a bill to revoke no-fault divorce in cases where one spouse opposes the divorce, and several other states are considering following Michigan's lead. Arguing that people "must begin to see the connection between divorce and other problems, especially poverty and juvenile delinquency," Jessie Dalman, the Republican sponsor of the Michigan bill, augmented the child-protection rationale with a direct appeal to women's fear of impoverishment.[61] Likewise, Dan Jarvis, director of the Michigan Family Forum policy group that has campaigned vigorously for this bill, portrayed it as protecting women: "Let's say a homemaker has a husband who cheats on her. Under the proposed law, she would have the upper hand. She can say: 'All right, you want your divorce? You can have it. But it's going to cost you.' "[62]

Many women—especially homemakers—and their children indeed have been impoverished by the unfair effects of current no-fault divorce property settlements, as feminist scholars and lawyers have documented.[63] The current unjust economic consequences of no-fault divorce laws is a serious problem in need of serious legislative and judicial reforms. It is a postfeminist sleight-of-hand, however, to pretend that repeal of no-fault divorce is the only or best possible remedy, or that it will promote greater gender equality in marriage. The rhetoric against no-fault erroneously implies that men seek a disproportionate number of contemporary divorces and that women have greater interests than men in sustaining their marriages. Unfortunately, the reverse is closer to the truth. Women seek a disproportionate number of contemporary divorces, despite the unjust consequences they risk in doing so, often because they find the injustices and difficulties of their marriages even harder to bear.[64]

Whether revisionist efforts to affix a tepid norm of gender equality to family-values rhetoric are well-intentioned or disingenuous, their marriage seems ill-fated. Principles of egalitarianism and stability frequently collide, and, as in too many traditional marriages, the former are sacrificed to the latter. Revisionists, unlike both orthodox family-values advocates and feminists, rarely confront a disturbing contradiction at the heart of the Western ideal of a fully volitional marriage system—historically, stable marriage systems have rested upon coercion, overt or veiled, and on inequality. Proposals to restrict access to divorce implicitly recognize this unpleasant contradiction, one which poses a thorny dilemma for a democracy. If, as many feminists fear, a stable marriage system depends upon systemic forms of inequality, it will take much more than moralistic jeremiads bemoaning family decline, or even mandatory waiting and counseling prerequisites to divorce, to prop up contemporary marital stability.

This bleaker, feminist analysis of contemporary marital fragility, rather than the "family optimism" which revisionists attribute to social scientists who do not share their views,[65] explains some of the political passions at stake in our dispute. Without coercion, as Wilson concedes, divorce and single motherhood rates will remain high. Indeed, I agree with Popenoe that women's capacity to survive outside marriage, however meagerly, explains why both rates rose so sharply in recent decades. Marriage became increasingly fragile as it became less economically obligatory, particularly for women. These developments expose the inequity and coercion that always lay at the vortex of the supposedly voluntary, "companionate marriage" of the traditional nuclear family. It seems a poignant commentary on the benefits to women of that family system that, even in a period when women retain primary responsibility for maintaining children and other kin, when most women continue to earn significantly less than men with equivalent cultural capital, and when women and their children suffer substantial economic decline after divorce, that in spite of all this, so many regard divorce as the lesser of evils.

I do not dispute Glenn's judgment that "male-female equality in a society in which the quality of life is mediocre for everyone is hardly anyone's idea of utopia."[66] However, perhaps because I am less willing to sacrifice women's precarious gains on the chimerical altar of social stability, I am more motivated to find alternative social responses to our misdiagnosed familial ills.

2. The "Biology" of Heterosexism   Homophobia also plays a closeted role in the centrist campaign, one that could prove more insidious than right-wing gay-bashing. Wilson includes popular discomfort with same-sex marriage in his sympathetic inventory of the family values of "reasonable people."[67] Popenoe makes one foray at a definition of the family broad enough to encompass "homosexual couples, and all other family types in which dependents are involved," only to retreat instantly to the linguistic mantra favoring "two biological parents" that pervades revisionist rhetoric.[68] Moynihan's conviction that children need to grow up in families that provide them with a "stable relationship to male authority," is echoed by Whitehead's undocumented claim that research demonstrates "the importance of both a mother and a father in fostering the emotional well-being of children."[69] Blankenhorn, once again, goes even further by explicitly condemning lesbian childbearing. Indeed his book formally proposes restricting access to donor sperm and alternative insemination services exclusively to married couples with fertility problems. "In a good society," Blankenhorn maintains, "people do not traffic commercially in the production of radically fatherless children."[70]

Elshtain unapologetically concedes that when she and her colleagues affirm a heterosexual family model, "we are privileging relations of a particular kind in which certain social goods are at stake."[71] Doing so panders to popular heterosexist prejudice. Despite consistent research findings that lesbians and gays parent at least as successfully as heterosexuals (see chapter five),[72] the Council on Families in America refuses to advocate equal marriage, adoption, or childbearing rights for the former. Rather, these self-described challengers of "ideological constraints" remain faithful to Etzioni's credo: "there are some issues, such as abortion and gay rights, that we know communitarians cannot agree on, so we have completely avoided them."[73]

Such evasion abets the social agenda and political strategy of organized reactionaries. Homophobia has become the wedge issue of the new right family warriors. When Republicans sought to scuttle passage of the Family Leave Act in January 1993, newly inaugurated Clinton's own first family-values offering, they did so by attempting to saddle it with a rider to prevent lifting the ban on gays in the military. Likewise, Falwell seized upon Clinton's nomination of a lesbian to an undersecretary post as an opportunity to flood the coffers of his Liberty Alliance. Urging readers to send donations of twenty-five dollars with a "Stop the Lesbian Nomination Reply Form," Falwell warned that, "President Clinton's nomination of Roberta Achtenberg, a lesbian, to the Department of Housing and Urban Development is a threat to the American family. . . . Achtenberg has dedicated her life to winning the "rights" of lesbians to adopt little babies. Please help me stop her nomination."[74] The Traditional Values Coalition, based in Anaheim, claims to have sold 45,000 copies of the videotape, "Gay Rights, Special Rights," that they designed expressly to mobilize anti-gay sentiment among African-Americans.[75] In March of 1996, Randall Terry, director of

Operation Rescue, the extreme right-wing, antiabortion group, flew to Hawaii to initiate a direct action campaign against the state court's anticipated legalization of gay marriage.

Ironically, the identification of Republicanism with such intolerance, with the notion, as Representative Constance Morella of Maryland puts it, that, "if you don't talk a certain way, raise your kids a certain way, love a certain way and pray a certain way, you are most certainly not welcome here," alarms many Party moderates. However, a forum they convened in May of 1993 to reorient the Party foundered on just this faultline, with conservatives supporting Buchanan's view that "traditional values is the last trump card the Republican Party possesses."[76] Centrist ideology colludes with a homophobic, right-wing agenda at a dangerous moment.

3. Making a "Career" of Class Bias   Less obvious than the gender and sexual stakes of family-values rhetoric, perhaps, are ways it also serves as a sanitized decoy for less reputable prejudices of class and race. Having studied working-class families struggling to sustain body, soul, and kin ties in the economically depressed Silicon Valley during the mid-1980s, I cannot help but wonder what sort of family bubble world revisionists like Whitehead, Popenoe, and other communitarians inhabit. Perhaps, their moralistic images of selfish, hedonistic adults who place their own emotional and sexual pleasures and career ambitions above the needs of their vulnerable children, derive from observations of some occupants who reside in a professional-corporate social cocoon.

Such caricatures bear little resemblance to twenty-something Carole, a laid-off electronics assembler and Fotomat envelope stuffer, a wife and mother of four, who left and returned to her abusive husband before she died of cancer. Nor do they apply to Lanny, another twenty-something, laid-off drafter, who divorced the substance-abusing father of her young daughter after discovering he had "snorted away" the down payment she had laboriously accumulated to purchase a house. They do not fit Jan, a forty-year-old lesbian social-service worker, who continues to contribute time, resources, and love to the son of a former lover. They do not adequately depict the hard choices or the family realities that confront any of the women I studied, or, I would venture, those of the vast majority of citizens. The idiom of careers that family-values enthusiasts employ suggests ignorance of how few adults in this postindustrial age enjoy the luxury of joining a new familism by choosing to place their children's needs above the demands of their jobs. They could win much more respect for their cause, and enhance its prospects, if they would spend nearly as much time badgering public and corporate leaders to provide citizens with the kinds of jobs, incomes, schedules, and working conditions that might make the practice of any reasonable sort of familism viable as they have devoted to persuading individuals that "the most important thing to change is our minds."[77]

4. **Willie Horton in Whiteface**   Wherever class bias flourishes, in the United States race can seldom be far behind, for, in our society, these two axes of injustice are always hopelessly entangled. Quayle's attack on Murphy Brown was an ill-fated attempt to play the Willie Horton card in whiteface. Without resorting to overtly racist rhetoric, the image conjured up frightening hordes of African-American welfare "queens" rearing infant fodder for sex, drugs, and videotaped uprisings, such as had just erupted in Los Angeles. As anthropologist Elizabeth Traube points out, "shadow traces of African-American family practices are inscribed in postfeminist visions of the family," and "Murphy Brown" directly exploits symbolic effects of this ancestry with its opening theme Motown soundtrack.[78] Lurking in Murphy's shadows were descendents of the pathological "black matriarchs" Moynihan had permanently etched into the collective consciousness nearly three decades ago.[79]

In case anyone in fin-de-siècle U.S.A. remained ignorant of the racial coding of family-values discourse, Charles Murray used a megaphone to teach them a crash course. His *Wall Street Journal* op-ed, reprinted by the *Philadelphia Enquirer* under the title "The

Emerging White Underclass and How to Save It," warned whites that their family patterns now resemble that malignant "tangle of pathology" which Moynihan presciently diagnosed in 1965 among African Americans. Displaying greater honesty than most revisionists, Murray concluded by speaking the unspeakable: "The brutal truth is that American society as a whole could survive when illegitimacy became epidemic within a comparatively small ethnic minority. It cannot survive the same epidemic among whites."[80]

Racial anxiety runs as subtext to the entire history of family-crisis discourse in the United States, which long predates Moynihan's incendiary 1965 report. It reaches back a century to xenophobic fears that, in the face of high fertility among eastern and southern European migrants, native white women, whose birth rates were declining were threatening their tribe with "race suicide." It reaches back much further into the history of colonial settler fears of the diverse sexual and kinship practices of indigenous cultures, as well as to rationales that esteemed, white scholars offered for African-American slavery—that it helped civilize the heathen by teaching family values to a species which lacked these. Consider that, until E. Franklin Frazier published *The Negro Family in the United States* in 1939, most social scientists subscribed to the view of Howard Odum that, "in his home life, the Negro is filthy, careless, and indecent . . . as destitute of morals as many of the lower animals . . . [and with] little knowledge of the sanctity of home or marital relations."[81] And this about a system that denied slaves the right to legal, or permanent, conjugal and parental bonds.

If marriage was a form of racial privilege under slavery, it is rapidly becoming so again today. Sociologist William Wilson has constructed a chauvinistic, but still stunning, "marriageable Black male index" that graphs the increasing scarcity of Black men who are neither unemployed nor incarcerated. Wilson's index indirectly demonstrates that male breadwinning and marriage are becoming interactive badges of race and class status.[82] Indeed, the greatest contrast in family patterns and resources in the U.S. today is between two

steady-earner and single-mother households, and these divide notably along racial lines. No doubt this is why Presidential voting patterns in 1992 displayed a family gap more pronounced than the
gender gap. Married voters heavily favored Bush, while the unmarried shored Clinton's precarious margin of victory.[83] A campaign
that sets couple- and single-parent families at odds has political consequences. Centrist Democrats hope to erode the advantage Republicans enjoy among the largely white, middle-class, heterosexual,
two-parent family set.

The Emerging Conservative Cultural "Consensus"

Such a strategy is unlikely to succeed. As leaders of the right-wing
Christian profamily movement recognize, with delight, family-values
ardor more readily promotes their reactionary agenda. Gary Bauer,
president of the right-wing Family Research Council and editor of
the fundamentalist *Focus on the Family Citizen*, gloats that there are
encouraging "signs that a pro-family consensus, which has been
forming for several years, is continuing to gel," despite the election
of Clinton. Identifying the *Atlantic* as the premier organ "of smug,
elitist, knee-jerk liberalism," Bauer aptly reads Whitehead's vindica-
tion of Quayle as the most prominent of increasing "signs that the
traditionalist revival among policy experts has not been snuffed
out."[84]

Bauer understands the political implications of neo-family values
discourse far better than do its propagators. Despite the collectivist
aspirations of communitarian ideology, the political effects of identifying family breakdown as the crucible of all the social crises that
have accompanied postindustrialization and the globalization of capitalism are privatistic and profoundly conservative. Clinton's own
welfare reform proposals, which differed from those of the Republican right-wing only in their lesser degree of severity rather than in
their ideological presumptions about family breakdown and welfare
dependency, should be persuasive on this score.

Particularly troubling, and ironic, has been the success of recent appeals to homophobic family values among African-American ministers-and the electorate they influence. In November 1993, the religious right succeeded in winning support for repeal of a local gay rights protection ordinance from 56 percent of the voters in traditionally liberal black precincts in Cincinnati. Effectively portraying the gay and lesbian movement "as a group of well-off whites fighting for 'special rights,'" the right-wing family-values campaign convinced a majority of black voters that the interests and constituencies of the two movements are antagonistic.[85] Similar strategic alliances of right-wing family-values activists and African-American clergy blocked the passage of the first referendum for domestic partners legislation in San Francisco in 1989.

Thus the rush to consensus on family values is not only premature; it is undemocratic. The idea that we should all subscribe to a unitary ideal of family life is objectionable on social scientific, ethical, and political grounds. I had hoped, and Bauer and his associates had feared, that the 1992 electoral defeat of the right-wing family values campaign would signal an opportunity for democratic initiatives on family and social reforms, initiatives that would begin with a recognition of how diverse our families are and will continue to be. Instead, we have witnessed the startling resurrection of family-values ideology. Beneath its new, velvet gown is an old-fashioned, confining, one-size-fits-all corset. But our nation's families come in many shapes and sizes, and will continue to do so. A democratic family politics must address diverse bodily and spiritual desires in rhetoric people find at least as comfortable as the ever-popular, combat uniform of family values.

Toward Reconfiguring Family Values

No sound-bite rebuttal can convey the complex, contradictory character of family and social turmoil. Still, we must disrupt the stampede to premature consensus on family values. To wage a viable countercultural campaign for *social* values, progressives need to confront the impoverishment of our national capacity to imagine human bonds beyond familial ones that can keep individuals safe from a "heartless world." So atrophied is this cultural muscle that family impulses overcompensate.

Two media items illustrate the cultural ubiquity of this ideological translation. An op-ed by China scholar Franz Schurmann that lauded the cooperative, cultural traditions that have generated phenomenal economic growth in China concluded that "creating new *social power* is the key to reversing the United States' decline (my emphasis)." Not once did Schurmann use the ubiquitous "F" word, but the editorial page editor affixed the title "Families That Work Are Helping China."[86]

More predictable was the photo caption, "The Post-Nuclear Family," which the *New York Times* ran over a picture of young Black "doughnut men" (joyride car thieves) in Newark, New Jersey. The photo accompanied a story identifying family decline as the source of delinquency as well as the impetus for parental appeals to "government, schools and whatever communal vestiges remain in a mobile and complex society," for help in rearing law-abiding youth.[87]

We cannot counter the flawed, reductionist logic of family-values ideology, however, unless we resist using knee-jerk, symmetrical responses, like a feminist bumper sticker Whitehead cites effectively to mock feminism: "Unspoken Traditional Family Values: Abuse, Alcoholism, Incest."[88] Portraying nuclear families primarily as sites of patriarchal violence, as some feminists have done, is inaccurate and impolitic.[89] It reinforces a stereotypical association of feminism with anti-familism, which does not even accurately represent feminist perspectives on the subject. Certainly, protecting women's rights to resist and exit unequal, hostile, dangerous marriages remains a crucial project, but one we cannot advance by denying that many women, many of them feminists, sustain desires for successful and legally protected relationships with men and children. We must steer a tenuous course between cultural warriors who blame public violence on (patriarchal) family decline, and those who blame family decline on (patriarchal) domestic violence.

A better strategy is to work to redefine family values democratically by extending full rights, obligations, resources, and legitimacy to a diversity of intimate bonds. We might take our lead here from the only partly parodic family values campaign currently blossoming among gays and lesbians (see chapter five). Progressives could appeal to the rhetoric of the neo-family-values crusade in order to advocate full marital, reproductive, and custody rights for homosexuals. Such a strategy requires bridging the rift between gays and African Americans, first by disputing the erroneous notion that these are distinct communities, and second by addressing racism among white gays and black homophobia at the grassroots level. African American heterosexuals and all homosexuals, supported by a full-spectrum rainbow coalition, must come to recognize mutual interests in democratizing family rhetoric, rights, and resources.

Exposing the PMC (professional middle-class) bias of communitarian ideology, as sociologist Charles Derber has done, offers another opportunity to identify with the actual family needs of the vast majority of citizens.[90] However, we must first acknowledge that full-time homemaking, like the male family wage on which it depends, has become a form of class privilege that eludes increasing numbers of women to whom it appears, often legitimately, far preferable to the unsatisfying, poorly paid work to which they are consigned.[91] Unless feminism can shed its well-earned reputation for disdain toward the world of the full-time, cookie-baking mom, revisionists will effectively exploit feminist class prejudices.

Another way to reconfigure family values is to up the ante in the revisionist bid to elevate the cultural status and responsibilities of fatherhood. Here I agree with Blankenhorn that the sort of family values campaign we most urgently need is one to revise popular masculinities. Family-less fathers, be they married or single, do seem to be disproportionately harmful to women, children, and civil society, as well as to themselves. Normative masculine behavior among the overpaid ranks of greedy, competitive, corporate and professional absent fathers and also among more overtly macho, underpaid, underemployed, undereducated, volatile "boyz 'n the hood," can lead women, as well as men to idealize cinematic visions of Victorian patriarchy. We sorely need cultural efforts to deglamorize violence, predatory sexuality, and sexism, such as the one that was announced in 1994 by an organization of Black professional women. We also need to challenge the destructive androcentric logic behind "the clockwork of male careers."[92] Unfortunately, currently the most prominent initiatives of this sort—the Christian men's movement, Promise Keepers, and the African-American Million Man March that was called by Farrakhan—seem to share with Blankenhorn nostalgic affection for a world of "Father Knows Best." The democratic challenge is to find ways to affirm the laudable sentiments these movements tap while enticing them to follow a more egalitarian, "different drummer, marchers, please."[93]

Progressives might try to go further than revisionists in efforts to domesticate men. Why not promote full-time homemaking and childrearing as a dignified alternative to over-, under- and unemployment for men, as well as for women? Although the percentages remain small, increasing numbers of men have begun to find this a rewarding and challenging vocation. Popenoe, citing both Wilson and George Gilder and echoing even feminist Sherry Ortner, maintains that "men need the moral and emotional instruction of women more than vice versa, and family life, especially having children, is a considerable civilizing force for men."[94] If correct, then giving men full-time domestic obligations should prove a potent curriculum.

Rethinking family values requires dodging ideological corners into which revisionists deftly paint feminists and other progressives. First, we must concede that the best familial interests of women (or men) and children do not always coincide. While research demonstrates that high-conflict marriages are at least as destructive to children as is parental divorce, clearly there *are* some unhappy marriages whose adult dissatisfactions harm children much less than do their post-divorce circumstances. Certainly, some divorces *are* better for the adults who initiate them than for the children who must adjust to them. Ironically, joint custody arrangements often impose a particularly unfair burden on children of divorce. Joint custody preferences were adopted by many states along with no-fault divorce not only to foster greater gender equality for parenting adults, but also to serve children's interests in maintaining intimate relationships with both parents after a divorce. Unfortunately, the consequences have been far less benevolent. At their best, even amicable joint custody arrangements typically force children, rather than parents, to become residential commuters between two different households, neighborhoods, or even communities. At their worst, antagonistic joint custody situations extend indefinitely the exposure of children to the damaging effects of parental hostility and conflict. In consequence, so many women have bargained away economic support in order to retain primary custody of their children that some feminist lawyers are proposing to revise the custody standard applied in divorce custody conflicts. For example, University of California family law professor Carol Bruch is promoting legislation to replace the state's current judicial presumption in favor of joint custody awards with one that grants primary custody to the parent who actually had served as a child's primary caretaker prior to the divorce.[95]

Likewise, just as there are His and Her marriages, so too, divorce is often better for one spouse (not always the male) than the other, as are many remarriages and the stepfamilies they create. When the best interests of the genders collide, it is not easy to say whose should prevail. However, it is also not easy to say whether or not the genders actually do have incompatible interests in making all marriages harder to leave. The vast majority of women, men and their children derive clear benefits from living in loving, harmonious, secure relationships, but men and women in marriages like these rarely choose to divorce. What is really at issue in the great divorce controversy is the extent to which easy access to divorce encourages individuals to indulgently throw in the towel on marriages that are not too wet to be saved. In other words, how many marriages that now end in divorce could have been saved, and would have been better off for all parties if they had been?

Research does not, and probably cannot, shed much useful light on this question. No doubt "divorce culture," as critics call it, does foster some undesirable instances of capricious divorce. But, how large is that incidence, and at what cost do we deter it? Contrary to the claims of the anti-divorce campaigners, there is little evidence that many parents regard divorce as a casual, impulsive, or easy decision. Nor is there evidence that divorce restrictions are likely to achieve their intended effect of buttressing marital commitment. They are at least as likely to deter people from marrying in the first place, and more likely to encourage unhappily married individuals to resort to extra-legal forms of desertion and separation. These practices have become so widespread in Roman Catholic countries that even Ireland has taken measures to legalize divorce. For better and worse, governmental attempts to socially engineer the quality, as opposed to the legal form, of intimate relationships have an abysmal historical track record.

The campaign against single mothers calls for an analogous response. We do not need to defend single mothers from the open season of cultural bounty hunters by denying that two compatible, responsible, committed, loving parents generally *can* offer greater economic, emotional, physical, intellectual and social resources to their children than can one from a comparable cultural milieu. Of course, if two parents are generally better than one, three or four might prove better yet. A version of Barbara Ehrenreich's Swiftian proposal, that to lift their families out of poverty, Black women should wed, "Two, Three, Many Husbands,"[96] is unlikely to win popular affection. Still, we might draw upon communitarian sentiments to foster much more collective responsibility for children. Spontaneously, many childless and childfree adults are choosing to become unofficial para-parents, by forming nurturant, long-term relationships with the children of overburdened parents (a category from which few parents would exclude themselves). Children's advocates might actively promote and seek social protection for these voluntary extended kin relationships, which, as the *New York Times* put it, treat "children as a collective commitment that is more than biological in its impulse."[97] No doubt such proposals would prove more appealing and constructive than polyandry.

Similarly, we should not feel obliged to reject the claim that in industrial societies, teenage motherhood often does not augur well for the offspring. Without disputing the view that most teens today lack the maturity and resources to parent effectively, we might point out that this is at least as true of those whom Murray would shame and starve into shotgun marriages as of those who lack daddies or whose daddies lack shotguns. The rising age of marriage since the 1950s is a positive, rather than a negative trend, but one which leads to more nonmarital sexuality and pregnancies. Yet countries like Sweden, which do not stigmatize unwed births but make sex education, contraception, and abortion services widely and cheaply available to all, witness few unwanted births and few births to teen mothers. The misguided drive to restigmatize "illegitimacy," demands renewed struggle to destigmatize abortion among both the populace and health providers and to vastly increase its accessibility. A reinvigorated campaign for comprehensive reproductive rights, perhaps reviving that old Planned Parenthood slogan, "every child, a wanted child," should promote a full panoply of contraceptive options, like RU-486. It might include a take back our bodies drive to wrest exclusive control over abortion provision from doctors, particularly when so few of these in the U.S. have proven willing to subject their professional status, personal safety, perhaps even their lives, to the formidable risks that the anti-abortion movement imposes on abortion providers.[98] At the same time, we should resist the misrepresentation of feminism as hostile to motherhood or "life" by continuing the struggle for genuine, humane workplace and welfare reforms (rather than repeals) that make it possible for women to choose to mother or to reject maternity.

Feminists are particularly well placed to promote this humane brand of progressive family values. Unlike revisionists, we understand that it is not the family, but one, historically specific, system of family life (the "modern nuclear family") that has broken down. We understand, too, that this has had diverse effects on people of different genders, races, economic resources, sexual identities, and generations. Some have benefitted greatly; others have lost enormously; most have won a few new rights and opportunities and lost several former protections and privileges. The collapse of our former national consensus on family values, like the collapse of our prosperous economy to which it was intricately tied, has not been an equal opportunity employer. Indeed, women, especially poor and minority women, have been some of the biggest winners, and most of the biggest losers. Those who do not want to count feminism, liberalism, or human compassion, casualties of the emergent new consensus on neo-family values had better disrupt the mesmerizing, but misguided, campaign.

CHAPTER 4

Virtual Social Science and the Politics of Family Values

. . . .

From the wild Irish slums of the 19th-century Eastern seaboard to the riot-torn suburbs of Los Angeles, there is one unmistakable lesson in American history: a community that allows a large number of young men to grow up in broken families, dominated by women, never acquiring any stable relationship to male authority, never acquiring any set of rational expectations about the future—that community asks for and gets chaos. Crime, violence, unrest, unrestrained lashing out at the whole social structure—that is not only to be expected; it is very near to inevitable.

—*Daniel Patrick Moynihan, 1965*

The way a male becomes a man is by supporting his children. . . . What (the Democrats) cannot accept is that government proposals have failed. It is the family that can rebuild America. . . . The dissolution of the family, and in particular, the absence of fathers in the lives of millions of America's children is the single most critical threat (to our future).

—*Dan Quayle, September 8, 1994*

That is a disaster. It is wrong. And someone has to say again, "It
is simply not right. You shouldn't have a baby before you're
ready, and you shouldn't have a baby when you're not married."
           —*President Bill Clinton, September 9, 1994*

No doubt many of the social scientists who have regrouped outside
the academy to wage a secular campaign for family values sincerely
worry about the deteriorating welfare of our children and society.
Nonetheless, their extra-curricular efforts respond as well to major
shifts in the politics of knowledge within the academy. Just when the
postmodern family condition was supplanting the 1950s version of
the modern family system whose conventions and values continue to
haunt contemporary culture, so too were new approaches to knowledge challenging the ruling frameworks of modernist, 1950s social
science to which the family-values campaigners adhere. The gap in
the degree of prestige that modern family sociology now enjoys in
popular, as compared with professional, domains is also considerable, and growing. Meanwhile, fin-de-millennium politicians of dis-
parate ideological hues have come to perceive significant rewards in
family-values discourse, as the two excerpts above from back-to-back,
nearly interchangeable 1994 election season speeches by Dan Quayle
and President Clinton indicate. A peculiar conjuncture of political
and academic dislocations has opened the door for collaboration
between mainstream social scientists and electoral politicians. Revisionist family-values scholars are supplying substantial ideology, rhetoric, and legitimacy to post–Cold War "New" Democrats and the
vanishing species of "moderate" Republicans alike.

    Playing hooky from our besieged and tarnished ivory towers,
numerous social scientists, now including myself, are waging public
cultural combat, for weighty political stakes, over the sources of and
remedies to the fall of the modern family system. As the United
States approaches the third Christian millennium, the everyday practices and conditions of social and material decline are increasingly at
odds with a mythic discourse of family values.

A *Bedtime Fable for the American Century*

Once upon a fabulized time, half a century ago, there was a lucky land where families with names like Truman and Eisenhower presided over a world of Nelsons, Cleavers, and Rileys. Men and women married, made love and (in that proper order) produced gurgling, Gerber babies. It was a land where, as God and Nature had ordained, men were men and women were ladies. Fathers worked outside the home to support their wives and children, and mothers worked inside the home without pay to support their husbands and to cultivate healthy, industrious, above-average children. Streets and neighborhoods were safe and tidy. This land was the strongest, wealthiest, freest, and fairest in the world. Its virtuous leaders, heroic soldiers, and dazzling technology defended all the freedom-loving people on the planet from an evil empire which had no respect for freedom or families. A source of envy and inspiration, the leaders and citizens of this blessed land had good reason to feel confident and proud.

And then, as so often happens in fairy tales, evil came to this magical land. Sometime during the mid-1960s, a toxic serpent wriggled its way close to the pretty picket fences guarding those Edenic gardens. One prescient, Jeremiah Daniel Patrick Moynihan,[1] detected the canny snake and tried to alert his placid countrymen to the dangers of family decline. Making a pilgrimage from Harvard to the White House, he chanted about ominous signs and consequences of "a tangle of pathology" festering in cities that suburban commuters and their ladies-in-waiting had abandoned for the crabgrass frontier. Promiscuity, unwed motherhood, and fatherless families, he warned, would undermine domestic tranquility and wreak social havoc. Keening only to the tune of black keys, however, this Pied Piper's song fell flat, inciting displeasure and rebuke.

It seemed that overnight, those spoiled Gerber babies had turned into rebellious, disrespectful youth who spurned authority, tradition, and conformity, and scorned the national wealth, power, and imperial status in which their elders exulted. Rejecting their parents' gray flannel suits and Miss American ideals, as well as their monogamous, nuclear families, they generated a counterculture and a sexual revolution, and they built unruly social movements demanding student rights, free speech, racial justice, peace, liberation for women, and for homosexuals. Long-haired, unisex-clad youth smoked dope and marched in demonstrations shouting slogans like, "Question Authority," "Girls Say Yes to Boys Who Say No," "Smash Monogamy," "Black Is Beautiful," "Power to the People," "Make Love, Not War," "Sisterhood is Powerful," and "Liberation Now." Far from heeding Moynihan's warning, many young women drew inspiration from the "black matriarchs" he had condemned, condemning Moynihan instead for blaming the victims.

Disrupting families and campuses, the young people confused and divided their parents and teachers, even seducing some foolish elders into emulating their sexual and social experiments. But the thankless arrogance of these privileged youth, their unkempt appearance, provocative antics, and amorality also enraged many, inciting a right-wing, wishful, moral majority to form its own backlash social movement to restore family and moral order.

And so it happened that harmony, prosperity, security, and confidence disappeared from this once most fortunate land. After decimating Black communities, the serpent of family decline slithered under the picket fences, where it spewed its venom on white, middle-class families as well. Men no longer knew what it meant to be men, and women had neither time nor inclination to be ladies. Ozzie had trouble finding secure work. He was accused of neglecting, abusing, or oppressing his wife and children. Harriet no longer stayed home with the children. She too worked outside the home for pay, albeit less pay. Ozzie and Harriet sued for divorce. Harriet decided she could choose to have children with or without a marriage certificate, with or without an Ozzie, or perhaps even with a Rozzie. The clairvoyant Daniel Patrick Moynihan found himself vindicated at last, as political candidates from both ruling parties

joined his hymns of praise to Ozzie and Harriet Nelson and re-
buked the selfish family practices of their rebellious stepchild,
Murphy Brown.

The era of the modern family system had come to an end, and
few felt sanguine about the postmodern family condition that had
succeeded it. Unaccustomed to a state of perpetual instability and
definitional crisis, the populace split its behavior from its beliefs.
Many who contributed actively to such postmodern family statistics
as divorce, remarriage, blended families, single parenthood, joint
custody, abortion, domestic partnership, two-career households, and
the like still yearned nostalgically for the "Father Knows Best" world
they had lost. "Today," in the United States, as historian John Gillis
so aptly puts it, "the anticipation and memory of family means more
to people than its immediate reality. It is through the families we live
by that we achieve the transcendence that compensates for the tensions and frustrations of the families we live *with*."[2] Not only have the
fabled modern families we live *by* become more compelling than the
messy, improvisational, patchwork bonds of postmodern family life,
but as my bedtime story hints, because they function as pivotal elements in our distinctive national consciousness, these symbolic families are also far more stable than any in which future generations
ever dwelled.

Similar evidence of the decline of the modern family system
appears throughout the postindustrialized world, and for similar reasons, but thus far, in no other society has the decline incited responses so volatile, ideological, divisive, or so politically mobilized
and influential as in the US.[3] Only here, where the welfare state was
always underdeveloped and is now devolving, where religious fervor
and populist movements flourish and organized labor languishes, has
the beloved bedtime fable begun to evoke so many nightmares. Now
the crisis of family order incites acrimonious conflicts in every imag-
inable arena—from television sitcoms to Congress, from the Boy
Scouts of America to the United States Marines, from local school
boards to multinational corporations, from art museums to health

insurance underwriters, from Peoria to Cairo, and from political conventions to social science conferences.

Social Science Marching On

> Contrary to expectations many of you may have of historians, I'm not here to tell you that we have seen it all before. The current obsession with family values seems to me, if not entirely new, then peculiar to the late twentieth century, and I will argue that what we are experiencing is yet another dimension of what David Harvey has called the "postmodern condition," and example of what Anthony Giddens has identified as the late twentieth century capacity for intimacy at a distance.
>
> —*John Gillis, "What's Behind the*
> *Family Values Debate?"*

> The essential integrity of at least a large proportion of American family social scientists is evidenced by the fact that as the evidence accumulated on the effects of family changes, the originally sanguine views of the changes began to change to concern.
>
> —*Norval Glenn, "The Re-evaluation of Family*
> *Change by American Social Scientists"*

Just as no new family system has yet succeeded in attaining the status which the modern, male-breadwinner, nuclear family order enjoyed at mid-century, likewise the ruling intellectual frameworks of 1950s sociology have been dethroned, but not supplanted. Probably no academic discipline felt the disruptive impact of the social movements of the 1960s and early 1970s more strongly than sociology. Seeking to understand and critique their own society and to explore alternatives, activist students with left-wing commitments, including draft resisters in search of student deferments, entered sociology in droves. Infatuated with romantic versions of Marxism, Leninism, Trotskyism, Maoism, and other radical theories, radical young sociologists rejected most mainstream social theories as apologias for racism and imperialistic ventures and for the conformity and false promises of the Cold War era.

A feminist onslaught on the discipline pursued the left-wing attacks on modernization theory and on the functionalist theories of Talcott Parsons that justified the gender order of the modern family as functional for a modern industrial society. During the late 1960s and early 1970s, the grass roots women's movement spurred a wave of feminists to enter academic careers, where the liberal cast and the diffuse intellectual boundaries of sociology attracted many, like myself, to the discipline. Feminists organized professional caucuses, conferences, journals, and research sections in the American Sociological Association, rapidly transforming the demographics, intellectual preoccupations, and the leadership of both the professional organization and the discipline. The explicitly feminist Sex and Gender section, formed in the early 1970s, rapidly outdistanced the older, far more mainstream section on family sociology in membership, intellectual dynamism, and appeal. By 1993, it had become the largest research section in the A.S.A.[4]

Left-wing and feminist interventions challenged the value-free, scientific pretensions of sociology throughout the discipline, but few subfields were quite so dislocated as family sociology. During the mid-1970s, sociology of the family experienced what Canadian sociologist David Cheal terms, "a Big Bang in which feminism played a conspicuous part."[5] I share Cheal's view that the "explosion blew the field apart, and the separate pieces have been flying off in different directions ever since." The modernist sociology that Talcott Parsons and his colleagues practiced had posited the universality of the nuclear family and theorized that the gender structure of its male breadwinner-female homemaker genus evinced an ideally evolved, "functional fit" with modern industrial society and political democracy.[6] In 1963, sociologist William J. Goode's *World Revolution and Family Patterns* predicted that modernization would accomplish the global diffusion of the superior Western variety of family life and, thereby, of the democratic society it was thought to nurture.[7]

Feminist scholars, however, rapidly subjected 1950s families and family sociology alike to trenchant critique. Influenced by demographic evidence of rapid family transformations in the United States, by countercultural communal experiments and by the anti-housewife ethos of the early women's liberation movement, feminist scholars challenged the implicitly ethnocentric and androcentric foundations of the prevailing theories about family life. Betty Friedan's scathing attack on "the functionalist freeze" in *The Feminine Mystique* had directly launched such a project by blaming this brand of social science for entrapping overeducated, suburban homemakers in the "problem that has no name."[8] It was but a short leap from there to sociologist Jessie Bernard's academic work on His and Her marriages[9], or from incendiary movement classics like Pat Mainardi's "The Politics of Housework" and Ann Koedt's "The Myth of the Vaginal Orgasm," to scholarly treatments like Ann Oakley's *The Sociology of Housework* and Gayle Rubin's "The Traffic in Women."[10]

Meanwhile, outside the embattled groves of academe, a rightwing profamily movement rapidly polarized popular discourse on family change into feminist vs antifeminist, left vs right, and fundamentalist vs secular humanist camps. This forced the largely liberal ranks of mainstream family scholars, many of them predisposed to sympathize with Moynihan's earlier, ill-timed critique of "Negro family decay," to confront uncomfortable ideological choices.[11] Initially most accommodated their work to liberal feminist values, but the conditions under which they did so sowed seeds of resentment that would come full term in the backlash against political correctness of the 1990s. During the 1960s and 1970s most scholars in the subfield appeared to support liberal feminist critiques of the modern nuclear family. Many mainstream family scholars expressed a tolerant, relativistic stance toward various aspects of family experimentation and the sexual revolution of the time, and generally the findings of the studies they conducted on subjects like divorce, maternal employment, day care, single parenthood, and sexual experimentation gave comfort to the rising numbers of people involved in such practices.

Norval Glenn, a prominent senior family sociologist in the United States who is now a member of the Council on Families in America, surveyed this disciplinary history as participant-observer during lectures he delivered in 1994 in conjunction with the UN International Year of The Family. "Social scientists in the United States generally took a sanguine view of the family changes that started or accelerated in the mid-1960s. Although the label of "family decline" was often attached by social scientists to the family changes that occurred early in the century, the prevailing view in the 1960s and 1970s was that the family was only adapting to new circumstances, not declining."[12]

Sociologists in that period promoted a Pollyannish assessment of rising divorce rates, interpreting the trend both "as a sign that marriage had become more, not less, important," to adults, because they were no longer willing to settle for unhappy unions, and as beneficial in the long run for children released from the hostile environment of an unhappily married parental home.[13] Glenn claims that he and his colleagues felt "strongly inclined to express positive views of recent family changes," then, because the changes coincided with a feminist movement that "viewed family change and the trend toward gender equality as parts of the same bundle." "Being human," sociologists sought "the approval of those whose opinions matter to them, and those persons are largely liberals" who embrace "the ideal of male-female equality."[14] Andrew Cherlin, a prominent demographer and family sociologist whose work does not support the neo-family-values campaign, confirms this assessment of feminist influence on family sociologists: "It is above all the wish to avoid sounding like an antifeminist, I think, that causes liberals to downplay the costs of the recent trends."[15]

Since the late 1970s, however, the ideological force field within which scholars investigate the consequences of family change has become increasingly conservative. Speaking to prominent governmental, religious, and academic bodies in Australia, Glenn applauded social scientists for a voluminous "second thoughts" literature that recants earlier uncritical stances on family change, especially concerning the social effects of divorce, fatherlessness, and single motherhood. Psychologist Judith Wallerstein's widely popularized work[16], which finds that divorce inflicts substantial, lasting, and harmful effects on children, has been particularly influential, as has demographer Sara McLanahan's revised assessment that single-parent families harm children.[17] Adding his voice to "most of the more prominent family social science researchers," who, he claims, now evaluate such changes "in distinctly negative terms," Glenn recounts his personal conversion to the now, "virtually unanimous," social scientific view that, "the best family situation for children and adolescents is one in which there is a successful, intact marriage of the biological (or adoptive) parents," and that single-parent and stepfamilies are "far less than ideal."[18]

Whereas Glenn perceptively recognized that feminists and liberal ideology influenced social scientists' earlier, less critical appraisals of family change, he shifts to an "objectivist," scientific narrative to account for their more pessimistic verdicts in the 1990s. His tribute to "the essential integrity" of family social scientists (included in an above epigraph), claims that the weight of cumulative data compelled this intellectual conversion. I believe, in contrast, that just as during the 1960s and 1970s, reconfigurations of power and knowledge provide more illuminating explanations. The metamorphosis in the opinions of family scholars occurred as a New World Order of global capitalism and economic crisis brought the glory days of sociology as a discipline to a halt, while the modernist theories that had sustained its liberal, humanitarian ethos began to falter in postmodernist, neoliberal, and postfeminist currents.

If feminism unleashed a "Big Bang" in family sociology, postmodern theories have yet to provoke much more than a whimper.

Even though most family scholars are enmeshed in an ideological crisis over the meaning of family under postmodern conditions of patchwork intimacy, very few participate "in discussions about so-called postmodern conditions of society and thought".[19] Like most sociologists in the United States, they remain remote from these discourses, still wedded to a view of knowledge that considers the meaning of texts, images, and facts to transparently reflect an objective, external reality. Feminist sociologists, along with some European theorists like Michel Foucault, Anthony Giddens, and Pierre Bourdieu, and occasional visits from colleagues in other disciplines, like historian John Gillis, who spoke at a session on the family-values debate at the 1994 meetings of the American Sociological Association, provide mainstream sociologists with their principal, and often unwelcome, exposure to such questions.[20]

Fending off the intellectual challenge of Gillis's reading of postmodern family developments on the A.S.A. panel, for example, Popenoe resorted to an anti-intellectual, populist mode that has become widespread in the family-values campaign. Amidst lingering echoes of appreciative applause for Gillis's paper, Popenoe mounted the podium of the Hotel Bonaventure's cavernous auditorium in Los Angeles and declared, "I guess I'm the right wing here, but that's not true outside of sociology."[21] Popenoe positioned himself against the elite world of academia and with "most Americans [who] agree with what I just said, except for the liberal intelligentsia I've been battling."[22]

An apparent lack of awareness about the changed historical conditions for knowledge production in which we now operate renders many family social scientists, particularly senior white males, responsive to the rewards of the revisionist campaign. Since the 1970s, so many women have entered the discipline of sociology that we have begun to outnumber men in the profession, but the massive feminist Sex and Gender research section of the American Sociological Association remains a female ghetto — alien, unfamiliar territory to most mainstream family scholars.[23] Academic feminism has been institutionalized, thereby achieving some respectability, but also, as any student familiar with Max Weber's classical analysis of the routinization of charisma might have predicted, becoming less threatening.[24] It is not surprising that displaced male scholars might now feel freer to expel feminist perspectives they once had been force-fed and never fully digested.

Moreover, the collapse of communism has provoked a crisis in Marxism and a loss of faith in materialist explanations for social change, with particularly strong effects in sociology. The nation's generalized right-wing political shift, the diffusion of postfeminist culture[25] and the organized movement against "political correctness" in higher education have offered family scholars compelling incentives to hopscotch over challenges to academic family theory posed by the postmodern family condition to land directly into the public political fray.

The centrist campaign for family values allows displaced, formerly liberal scholars a means to reclaim positions of intellectual authority without appearing to be antifeminist. Adopting the postfeminist rhetoric of "a new familism," the campaign distances itself from reactionaries intent on restoring Ozzie and Harriet to the frayed upholstery of their suburban throne. New familism, in Glenn's formulation, represents, "a return to the belief that stable marriages, two-parent families, and putting children's needs before those of adults are desirable and important. It differs from the older familism in its espousal of male-female equality and the rejection of economic dependence as a basis for marital stability."[26] Migrating ideologically from Moynihan to Friedan and then even farther back than Friedan herself traveled when she published *The Second Stage* in 1982,[27] revisionists applaud tenuous signs "at the mass level" of a "return toward more traditional family values (excluding the ideal of male dominance)."[28]

A few social scientists have found the centrist campaign a route to considerable public influence, media celebrity, and even academic attention. For example, speaking at a symposium, "Gender

Equality, Children and the Family: Evolving Scandinavian and American Social Policy," at University of California, Berkeley in April of 1994, Popenoe acknowledged that his 1988 book, *Disturbing the Nest*, which criticizes the impact of social democratic policies on family change in Sweden, had received a chilly response from the Swedes: "My book did not start a dialogue in Sweden. I wasn't even invited back." As if to confirm Popenoe's self-report, prominent Scandinavian scholars and officials in attendance gave his critical analysis of Scandinavian family policy a dismissive response. Karin Stoltenberg, the Director General of the Norwegian Ministry of Children and Family Affairs, for example, termed "insane" Popenoe's belief that welfare-state policies were the source of rising divorce rates in the Nordic countries.[29] Likewise, an anti-intellectual polemic that Popenoe delivered at the August 1994 American Sociological Association Meetings in Los Angeles confronted nearly a solid wall of disapproval from co-panelists and the audience. Session organizer Frank Furstenberg, a prominent demographer and family sociologist in the United States, chastised Popenoe's "unhelpful us/them approach" to sociologists and the family values debate. In response, Popenoe portrayed most sociologists as out of touch with popular concerns and invited listeners sympathetic with his views to accompany him to a nearby conference sponsored by the Communitarian Network.

Since Popenoe became a major organizer of the centrist family-values campaign, he has been invited again and again to deliver his lament for family decline in venues that range from the "MacNeil-Leher News Hour" to the U.S. Department of Transportation, from the *New York Times* to the *Chronicle of Higher Education*, in addition to academic conferences and meetings such as at U.C., Berkeley and the American Sociological Association. Blankenhorn, who often claims the mantle of social science despite his lack of an advanced degree in any of the social science disciplines, has achieved even greater celebrity with the National Fatherhood Tour he launched in conjunction with the release of his 1995 book *Fatherless America*.

From "Oprah" to CNN's "Talkback," from the cover pages of *Time* magazine to syndicated feature stories in hundreds of local newspapers, Blankenhorn has blazed an extramural trail to academic podiums.[30] Likewise, the family-values campaign has offered Galston, Etzioni, and their colleagues access to extensive public and professional recognition. Etzioni's public campaign as founder and director of the communitarian movement, for example, coincided with his successful bid to become president of the A.S.A., and Galston took leave from his professorship at the University of Maryland to serve as Deputy Assistant to President Clinton until June of 1995.

The rhetoric of the few women scholars, like Jean Bethke Elshtain and Sylvia Hewlett, who are visibly active in the revisionist campaign, suggests that they harbor more personalized resentments against academic feminists. Hewlett has blamed the anti-maternalist ethos of early second-wave feminism for compounding the tribulations she suffered when she was a pregnant assistant professor of economics at Barnard College in the 1970s.[31] Elshtain complains, more plausibly, that she is "hooted out of the room" by feminists whenever she talks "about not ceding the issue of family values to the right."[32] In fact, few academic feminists do sympathize with Elshtain's support for heterosexual marital privilege or her disapproval of single motherhood. Feminists have personal and political stakes in these judgements as profound as Elshtain's, and so few respond to her public challenges with scholarly dispassion.[33]

It seems ironic, and in my view unlucky, that challenges to knowledge induced by radical family changes and by feminism, which decentered mainstream family social scientists within the academy, propelled quite a few of them onto center stage in the public sphere where they speak to the broad audiences feminists used to address. There, aloof from even the modest constraints of academic peer review, they deploy social scientific authority to influence political responses to postmodern family struggles by disseminating selective readings of the very kind of modernist research on family change that feminist and other critical sociologists imagined we had discredited. In an era of academic retrenchment when universities like the University of Rochester, Washington University, Yale University, and San Diego State University have abolished or slashed their sociology departments, it should not be surprising that podiums outside the ivy pastures beckon sociologists with more gratifying rewards. Modernist family social scientists (and pretenders, like Blankenhorn) can often enhance their academic status in the public domain, where they enjoy much more intellectual esteem and influence than do most postmodernist or feminist theorists.

They have developed an extramural social science apparatus with which they wage their cultural crusade for centrist family values. As we saw in the last chapter, through interlocking networks of think tanks, organizations, periodicals, and policy institutes, these social scientists have been constructing a virtual scholarly and popular consensus in the media in support of the very narrative about universal family values that succumbed to feminist and other forms of scrutiny in academia. Saturating the media-beltway world they have come to inhabit with the ideology of new familism, they misleadingly maintain that social science has confirmed Moynihan's warning about the socially destructive effects of single motherhood, illegitimacy, and fatherless families.

In reality, scholars do not now, and likely will not ever, achieve consensus on the relative significance that family structure, material circumstances, the quality of parental relationships, and psychological factors play in shaping children's lives. While it is true that most family sociologists do express some uneasiness over mounting rates of single parenthood, the predominant scholarly view is that single-parent families are more often the consequence than the cause of poverty, unemployment, emotional distress, and other negative correlates.[34] Ironically, a book about the history of family policy in Sweden by right-wing historian and family-values champion Allan Carlson criticizes Gunnar and Alva Myrdal for their "use and abuse of social science" in promoting the kinds of cutting edge social democratic family policies in their nation of which Carlson disap-

proves. Yet Carlson's critique of this practice applies at least as well
to the contemporary family-values campaign in the United States
that he supports: "In short, it is difficult to see social science in this
episode as little more than a new tool for rhetorical control and
political advantage. Weak and inconsistent data, confusion over
cause and effect, and avoidance of experimentation proved to be no
obstacles to the construction and implementation of policy."[35]

The contemporary family-values campaign in the United States,
which Carlson supports, mixes a flawed modernist framework with
an unsophisticated notion of culture. It presumes that the truth about
the relative merits and effects of diverse family structures—be they
intact married-couple families, stepfamilies, single-parent families,
extended families, adoptive families, not to mention gay families—is
straightforward, knowable, and extricable from its social, economic,
and political context. Although some revisionists, like Glenn, concede that at times (always past times), ideological and cultural convictions interfere with the capacity of social scientists to perceive this
truth and temporarily distort social scientific knowledge, truth and
virtue still triumph in the end. In this view, most social scientists are
sufficiently scientific to listen when the data speak to them in robust
and uniform tones.

A second dubious assumption of the family-values campaign is
that truth is timeless as well as singular: a happy marriage in the 1990s
is the same as one in the 1950s, and divorce has the identical, negative effects. Culture intervenes simply to affect the frequency of
these structures by rendering each more or less attractive or despised,
and by sustaining or subverting individual submission to a regime of
duty, propriety, and self-sacrifice. Culture functions as a grab-bag
category—a black hole ready to absorb all messy unexplained causes
and consequences. Here it trumps material circumstances, collective
struggles, and institutional constraints as the reason for the decline of
stable and happy marriages and families documented by rising rates
of divorce, unwed motherhood, and deadbeat dads. Culture becomes
an unproblematic, remarkably flexible category from which individuals, like savvy shoppers, can select timeless garments like marital

commitment, fidelity and responsibility and discard their unfashionable accessories—like male dominance.

Somewhat regretfully perhaps, most of the social scientists active in the centrist family-values campaign have accepted the demise of the 1950s-style, male breadwinner family and the likely permanence of some level of postmodern family instability, diversity, and change.[36] Recognizing that working mothers, at least, are "here to stay," they promote a new (post)familism that evades the power and justice conflicts embedded in family transformation.[37] Following the successful example set by right-wing intellectuals, centrist family social scientists have regrouped outside the academy to provide a middle course between ideologies of the religious right on one side and feminism and gay liberation on the other.[38] They proffer eager politicians a social science narrative to compete with naturalist and divine justifications for the contested modern gender and family regime.

Sitcom Sociology for a Disaffected Electorate

Post–Cold War politicians from both moribund parties have compelling cause to grasp at this outstretched academic hand. With a shrinking, increasingly cynical, electorate, one described in a study by the Times Mirror Center for the People and the Press[39] as, "angry, self-absorbed, and politically unanchored," the volatile balance of electoral power rests in the hands of those elusive, "neglected, middle-class" voters, who are disproportionately white.[40] The Democratic Party, weakened by the erosion of its traditional liberal and working-class base, has particularly urgent need to court this constituency. The neo-family-values campaign offers "New Democrats" a way to exploit the ideological stranglehold that religious, right-wing, profamily crusaders have secured on the Republican Party in their efforts to lure Reagan Democratic defectors back to the fold. As one political journalist quipped, "Democrats Find the Right's Stuff: Family Values."[41]

During the 1994 election season, Republicans, for their part, worked actively to shed the unpopular, intolerant, profamily image emblazoned on the national unconscious by their televised 1992 national convention. Dan Quayle, William Bennett, and even leaders of the right-wing Christian Coalition, retreated from the militant profamily rhetoric they had imposed on the 1992 party platform, such as hardline opposition to abortion and gay rights. Asked for his views on abortion and homosexuality just before he addressed the Christian Coalition in September 1994, Quayle told reporters, "That's their choice."[42] Bennett's speech to the Christian conference advised participants to constrain their homophobic passions: "I understand the aversion to homosexuality. But if you look in terms of damage to the children of America, you cannot compare the homosexual movement, the gay rights movement, what that has done in damage to what divorce has done to this society."[43] Quayle defended this political regression toward the mean in explicitly instrumental terms: "The political situation has changed in this country. There's not the political support to make it illegal, so we should focus on reducing the number of abortions, and we want to change attitudes."[44]

Mirror-image speeches delivered during the 1994 election season by Quayle and Clinton previewed campaign rhetoric for the last presidential election of the millennium as the electorate observes prime-time combat for the family-values crown. However, this is a riskier game show for the Democrats than for the Republicans. After all, President Clinton, son of Virginia Kelley's colorful postmodern marital history, competes with a credibility gap that his own dalliances exacerbate. Richard Sennett suggests that "the popular language of 'family values' and of 'values' per se is a barely disguised language of sexual prohibitions," which imagines "the breakdown of family values and community standards to be synonymous with sexual explicitness."[45] Voters overwhelmingly view Republicans rather than Democrats as defenders of this symbolic domain.[46]

The rhetoric of family values provides an infinitely malleable symbolic resource that is understandably irresistible to politicians from both major parties in the age of corporate-sponsored, mass-media politics. The vague, but resonant language of family values functions more like potent images than like verbal communications subject to rational debate. Little wonder, therefore, that Murphy Brown, (but not Candice Bergen), enjoyed star billing in the 1992 presidential campaign when Quayle castigated the sitcom heroine for glamourizing unwed motherhood. In a moment of supreme irony, anchorwoman Murphy took to the sitcom airwaves to chastise the former vice president for being out of touch with the problems of *real* families. Millions of voters watched this well-hyped episode and the ensuing responses to Murphy's sermon provided by Quayle and the small group of single mothers he had selected to join him in viewing this electoral spectacle, on camera.[47] Most political commentators at the time echoed the sitcom heroine's scorn for the vice president's inability to distinguish virtual from actual families. Because the Quayle-Brown spectacle underscored the message of the Republicans' 1992 nominating convention that the grand old party was out of touch with ordinary families, it assisted Clinton's slim margin of victory.

Breathtakingly soon, however, Dan Quayle began to enjoy the last laugh, as even President Clinton joined the "Dan Quayle was Right" brigades. Quayle's campaign against single mothers scored such a dramatic comeback victory over Clinton, the reputed comeback king, because the former vice president's campaign scriptwriters were quick to grasp the "virtual" rather than factual character of contemporary family-values talk. They recognized that Murphy Brown could function symbolically as a wayward stepdaughter of Ozzie and Harriet Nelson, the mythic couple who lodge, much larger than life, in collective nostalgia for the world of 1950s families.

The 1950s was the moment of origin of the fable of virtual family values. Those halcyon days of the modern nuclear family were also the years when television became a mass medium, indeed an obligatory new member of "the family." From its hallowed living room perch, the magic box broadcast the first generation of domestic sitcoms, emblazoning idealized portraits of middle-class family dynamics into the national unconscious. From "Ozzie and Harriet" to "Murphy Brown," from "Amos and Andy" to "The Cosby Show," from "The Life of Riley" to "Roseanne," the world of TV sitcoms saturates popular imagery of family life. Ozzie and Harriet and their kin serve as the Edenic families of our century's bedtime fable, because the apogee of the modern family system coincided with television's own origins and Golden Age.

Family sitcom programming was created in the post–World War II period to construct a mass viewing audience for the nascent television industry and its corporate sponsors. The programs did not simply reflect, or even just romanticize, the existing structure and values of the family audience they sought to entertain. Rather, as cultural historians have demonstrated, the introduction of television played an active role in constructing, and later in deconstructing, the boundaries of the isolated nuclear family it depicted in such sentimental tones.[48] Because the 1950s was also the first Cold War decade, the years when the United States emerged as the dominant global superpower, images of an invincible family and nation mingle inextricably in national imagery of the "good old days."[49] Clinton, Quayle, Newt Gingrich, and the primary constituencies of the electorate they address, as well as many of their academic counselors, all were reared in the first generation of families who learned to spend their evening hours huddled alone together in their families, watching family TV, in their newly conceived, "family rooms," designed as small shrines for the magic box.

This semiotic history of family sitcom TV, which evolved while the modern family it celebrated devolved, renders the idiom of family values a potent, inescapably visual and emotional register. Addressing emotional, rather than rational, frequencies, family-values discourse offers politicians and populace a brilliant defense mechanism with which to displace anxieties over race, gender, sexual, and class antagonisms that were unleashed as the modern family regime collapsed. No wonder that as the century ends, "it's all in the family."

During the 1994 and 1996 political seasons, the most popular sitcom social science script furnishes simple, emotionally resonant motivations and resolutions for those spectacles of routine fin-de-siècle violence, crime, and social decay that the networks broadcast nightly. Serial killers, crack babies, gang rapists, carjackers, dope dealers, drive-by shooters, school dropouts, welfare queens, arsonists, wifebeaters, child abusers, sex offenders, kidnappers, runaways, pregnant teens, gang warriors, homeless vagrants, terrorists—all social pathologies begin in a broken home. Her parents divorced, or they never married. His mother was hooked on welfare and drugs, or she dumped him in daycare. No one taught them family values. We need to stop coddling these criminals and con artists. From the punitive, anti-crime fervor of "three strikes and you're out" to "two tykes and you're out" welfare caps, family-values ideology plays to the privatistic, anti-government sentiments and the moralistic and vindictive appetites of our dismal, late millennial political culture.

An improbable alliance of academic and political networks produce and sponsor this sitcom sociology which is increasingly discordant with the diverse images of family life that now characterize contemporary domestic sitcom programs. Fending off competing political networks on the channels to their right and their left, mainstream family scholars and electoral candidates hope to keep the public tuned to the center of the political dial. Unwilling or unable to analyze the social sources of postmodern family and civic disorder, or to address the manifold injustices these upheavals expose and intensify, they resort to reruns of old family favorites. Religious and naturalist treatments of virtuous family order continue to play to substantial numbers of viewers in their specialized market niches. However, aging scholars, allied with New Democrats and moderate Republicans alike, have hitched their hopes for robust Nielson and ballot-box ratings to narratives featuring a prodigal society returning to conjugal family virtue after suffering the painful consequences of self-indulgent rebellions. The production company has assembled a postmodern pastiche of social science, fable, advanced technology and (dis)simulation to script and enact the serial melodrama. The plot-line, imagery, and production values owe more to television archives, and to power and knowledge shifts in the academy, economy, and polity, than they do to ethnographic or analytical acumen. This is the season for sitcom sociology—an effort to distract a disaffected public from the dire familial and social realities that the United States confronts as an ignoble century expires.

CHAPTE

Gay and Lesbian Families Are Here; All Our Families Are Queer; Let's Get Used to It! [1]

. . . .

In 1992 in Houston, I talked about the cultural war going on for the soul of America. And that war is still going on! We cannot worship the false god of gay rights. To put that sort of relationship on the same level as marriage is a moral lie.

—Pat Buchanan, February 10, 1996

Homosexuality is a peculiar and rare human trait that affects only a small percentage of the population and is of little interest to the rest.

—Jonathan Rauch 1994

I came to Beijing to the Fourth World Conference of Women to speak on behalf of lesbian families. We are part of families. We are daughters, we are sisters, we are aunts, nieces, cousins. In addition, many of us are mothers and grandmothers. We share concerns for our families that are the same concerns of women around the world.

—Bonnie Tinker, Love Makes a Family, September 1995

rt time ago, gay and lesbian families seemed quite a
ept, even preposterous, if not oxymoronic, not only to
and the general public, but even to most lesbians and gay
The grass roots movement for gay liberation that exploded into
blic visibility in 1969, when gays resisted a police raid at the
Stonewall bar in New York City, struggled along with the militant
feminist movement of that period to liberate gays and women *from*
perceived evils and injustices represented by the family, rather than
for access to its blessings and privileges. During the early 1970s,
marches for gay pride and women's liberation flaunted provocative,
countercultural banners, like "Smash The Family" and "Smash Monogamy." Their legacy is a lasting public association of gay liberation
and feminism with family subversion. Yet how "queer" such anti-
family rhetoric sounds today, when gays and lesbians are in the thick
of a vigorous profamily movement of their own.

Gay and lesbian families are indisputably here. In June of 1993,
police chief Tom Potter joined his lesbian, police officer daughter in
a Portland, Oregon gay pride march for "family values." By the late
1980s an astonishing "gay-by boom" had swelled the ranks of children living with gay and lesbian parents to between six to fourteen
million.[2] *Family Values* is the title of a popular 1993 book by and
about a lesbian's successful struggle to become a legal second mother
to one of these "turkey-baster" babies, the son she and his biological
mother have co-parented since his birth.[3] In 1989 Denmark became
the first nation in the world to legalize a form of gay marriage, termed
"registered partnerships," and its Nordic neighbors, Norway and Sweden soon followed suit. In 1993, thousands of gay and lesbian couples
participated in a mass wedding ceremony on the Washington Mall
during the largest demonstration for gay rights in U.S. history. Three
years later, on March 25, 1996, Mayor of San Francisco Willie Brown
proudly presided over a civic ceremony to celebrate the domestic
partnerships of nearly 200 same-sex couples. "We're leading the way
here in San Francisco," the mayor declared, "for the rest of the
nation to fully embrace the diversity of people in love, regard-

less of their gender or sexual orientation."[4] By then thousands of gay and lesbian couples across the nation were eagerly awaiting the outcome of "Baehr v. Lewin," cautiously optimistic that Hawaii's Supreme Court will soon order the state to become the first in the United States, and in the modern world, to grant full legal marriage rights to same-sex couples. As this book went to press in May 1996, the Republican party had just made gay marriage opposition a wedge issue in their presidential campaign.

Gay and lesbian families are undeniably here, yet they are not queer, if one uses the term in the sense of "odd" to signify a marginal or deviant population.[5] It is nearly impossible to define this category of families in a manner that could successfully distinguish all of their members, needs, relationships, or even their values, from those of all other families. In fact, it is almost impossible to define this category in a satisfactory, substantive way at all. What should count as a gay or lesbian family? Even if we bracket the thorny matter of how to define an individual as gay or lesbian and rely on self-identification, we still face a jesuitical challenge. Should we count only families in which every single member is gay? Clearly there are not very many, if even any, of these. Or does the presence of just one gay member color a family gay? Just as clearly, there are very many of these, including those of Ronald Reagan, Colin Powell, Phyllis Schlafly and Newt Gingrich.[6] More to the point, why would we want to designate a family type according to the sexual identity of one or more of its members? No research, as we will see, has ever shown a uniform, distinctive pattern of relationships, structure, or even of "family values," among families that include self-identified gays. Of course, most nongays restrict the term gay family to units that contain one or two gay parents and their children. However, even such families that most commonsensically qualify as gay or lesbian are as diverse as are those which do not.

Gay and lesbian families come in different sizes, shapes, ethnicities, races, religions, resources, creeds, and quirks, and even engage in diverse sexual practices. The more one attempts to arrive at a coherent, defensible sorting principle, the more evident it becomes that the category "gay and lesbian family" signals nothing so much as the consequential social fact of widespread, institutionalized homophobia.[7] The gay and lesbian family label marks the cognitive dissonance, and even emotional threat, that much of the nongay public experiences upon recognizing that gays can participate in family life at all. What unifies such families is their need to contend with the particular array of psychic, social, legal, practical, and even physical challenges to their very existence that institutionalized hostility to homosexuality produces. Paradoxically, the label "gay and lesbian family" would become irrelevant if the nongay population could only "get used to it."

In this chapter I hope to facilitate such a process of normalization, ironically, perhaps, to allow the marker "gay and lesbian" as a family category once again to seem queer—as queer, that is, as it now seems to identify a *family*, rather than an individual or a desire, as heterosexual. I conclude this book with an extensive discussion of this historically novel category of family, not only because of its inherent interest, but to suggest how it crystallizes the general processes of family diversification and change that characterize what I have been describing as the postmodern family condition.[8] Gay and lesbian families represent such a new, embattled, visible and necessarily self-conscious, genre of postmodern kinship, that they more readily expose the widening gap between the complex reality of postmodern family forms and the simplistic modern family ideology that still undergirds most public rhetoric, policy and law concerning families.[9] In short, I hope to demonstrate that, contrary to Jonathan Rauch's well-meaning claim in the second epigraph above, the experience of "homosexuals"[10] should be of immense interest to everyone else. Nongay families, family scholars and policymakers alike can learn a great deal from examining the experience, struggles, conflicts, needs, and achievements of contemporary gay and lesbian families.

Brave New Family Planning

History rarely affords a social scientist an opportunity to witness during her own lifetime the origins and evolution of a dramatic, and significant, cultural phenomenon in her field. For a family scholar, it is particularly rare to be able to witness the birth of an historically unprecedented variety of family life. Yet the emergence of the genus gay and lesbian family as a distinct social category, and the rapid development and diversification of its living species, have occurred during the past three decades, less than my lifetime. Of course, same-sex desire and behavior have appeared in most human societies, including all Western ones, as well as among most mammalian species; homosexual relationships, identities, and communities have much longer histories than most Western heterosexuals imagine; and historical evidence documents the practice of sanctioned and/or socially visible same-sex unions in the West, as well as elsewhere, since ancient times.[11] Nonetheless, the notion of a gay or lesbian family is decidedly a late twentieth-century development, and several particular forms of gay and lesbian families were literally inconceivable prior to recent developments in reproductive technology.

Indeed, before the Stonewall rebellion, the family lives of gays and lesbians were so invisible, both legally and socially, that one can actually date the appearance of the first identifiable species of gay family life—a unit that includes at least one self-identified gay or lesbian parent and children from a former, heterosexual marriage. Only one child custody case in the United States reported before 1950 involved a gay or lesbian parent, and only five more gays or lesbians dared to sue for custody of their children between 1950 and 1969. Then, immediately after Stonewall, despite the predominantly anti-family ethos of the early gay liberation period, gay custody conflicts jumped dramatically, with fifty occurring during the 1970s and many more since then.[12] Courts consistently denied parental rights to these early pioneers, rendering them martyrs to a cause made visible by their losses. Both historically and numerically, formerly married lesbian and gay parents who "came out" after marriage and secured at least shared custody of their children represent the most significant genre of gay families. Such gay parents were the first to level a public challenge against the reigning cultural presumption that the two terms—gay and parent—are antithetical. Their family units continue to comprise the vast majority of contemporary gay families and to manifest greater income and ethnic diversity than other categories of gay parents. Moreover, studies of their "care and feeding habits" provide nearly the entire data base of the extant research on the effects of gay parenting on child development.

It was novel, incongruous, and plain brave for lesbian and gay parents to struggle for legitimate family status during the height of the anti-natalist, anti-maternalist, anti-family fervor of grass-roots feminism and gay liberation in the early 1970s. Fortunately for their successors, such fervor proved to be quite short-lived. Within very few years many feminist theorists began to celebrate women's historically developed nurturing capacities, not coincidentally at a time when aging, feminist baby-boomers had begun producing a late-life boomlet of our own.[13] During the middle to late seventies, buoyed by the legacy of sexual revolution and feminist assertions of female autonomy, inspired by the "Black matriarchs" who had been turned into political martyrs by Daniel Patrick Moynihan's mid-sixties attack,[14] and abetted by the popularization of alternative reproductive technologies and strategies, a first wave of "out" lesbians began to join the burgeoning ranks of women actively choosing to have children outside of marriage.

Fully intentional childbearing outside of heterosexual unions represents one of the only new, truly original, and decidedly controversial genres of family formation and structure to have emerged in the West during many centuries. While lesbian variations on this cultural theme include some particularly creative reproductive strategies, they nonetheless represent not deviant, but vanguard manifestations of much broader late twentieth century trends in Western family life. Under postmodern conditions, processes of sexuality, con-

ception, gestation, marriage, and parenthood, which once appeared
to follow a natural, inevitable progression of gendered behaviors and
relationships, have come unhinged, hurtling the basic definitions of
our most taken-for-granted familial categories—like mother, father,
parent, offspring, sibling, and, of course, "family" itself—into cultural confusion and contention.

A peculiar melange of contradictory social forces, from the conservative turn to profamily and postfeminist sensibilities of the
Reagan-Bush era to the increased institutionalization, visibility, and
confidence of gay and lesbian communities, helped to fuel the "gay-
by" boom that escalated rapidly during the 1980s. It seems more
accurate to call this a "lesbaby boom," because lesbians vastly outnumber the gay men who can, or have chosen to, become parents
out of the closet. Lesbian planned parenthood strategies have spread
and diversified rapidly during the past two decades. With access to
customary means to parenthood denied or severely limited, lesbians
must necessarily construct their chosen family forms with an exceptional degree of reflection and intentionality. Accordingly lesbians
have been choosing motherhood within a broad array of kinship
structures. Like infamous Murphy Brown, some become single
moms, but more often lesbians choose to share responsibility for
rearing children with a lover and/or with other co-parents, such as
sperm donors, gay men, and other friends and relatives. New Hampshire and Florida categorically prohibit adoptions by lesbians or gay
men, and most adoption agencies actively discriminate against prospective gay parents. Consequently, independent adoption provided
the first, and remains the most traveled, route to lesbian maternity,
but increasing numbers of lesbians have been choosing to bear children of their own. In pursuit of sperm, some lesbians have resorted
quite instrumentally to heterosexual intercourse, but most prefer
alternative insemination strategies, locating known or anonymous
donors through personal networks or through private physicians or
sperm banks.

In the very period when the right-wing, profamily war against abortion has commanded center-ring priority in feminist struggles for reproductive rights, lesbians have had to apply considerable pluck and ingenuity in their own profamily efforts to procreate. Institution-alized heterosexism and married couple biases pervade the medically mediated fertility market. Most private physicians and many sperm banks in the United States, as well as the Canadian and most Euro-pean health services, refuse to inseminate unmarried women in gen-eral, and lesbians particularly. More than 90 percent of U.S. physicians surveyed in 1979 denied insemination to unmarried women, and a 1988 federal government survey of doctors and clinics reported that homosexuality was one of their top four reasons for refusing to provide this service.[15] Thus, the first wave of planned lesbian pregnancies depended primarily upon donors located through personal networks, frequently involving gay men or male relatives who might also agree to participate in childrearing, in vary-ing degrees. Numerous lesbian couples solicit sperm from a brother or male relative of one woman to impregnate her partner, hoping to buttress their tenuous legal, symbolic, and social claims for shared parental status over their "turkey-baster babies."

Despite its apparent novelty, "turkey-baster" insemination for infertility dates back to the late eighteenth century, and, as the nick-name implies, is far from a high-tech procedure requiring medical expertise.[16] Nonetheless, because the AIDS epidemic and the emer-gence of child custody conflicts between lesbians and known sperm donors led many lesbians to prefer the legally sanitized, medical route to anonymous donors, feminist health care activists mobilized to meet this need. In 1975 the Vermont Women's Health Center added donor insemination to its services, and in 1980 the Northern California Sperm Bank opened in Oakland expressly to serve the needs of unmarried, disabled, or nonheterosexual women who want to become pregnant. The clinic ships frozen semen throughout North America, and more than two-thirds of the clinic's clients are not married.[17]

The absence of a national health system in the United States commercializes access to sperm and fertility services, introducing an obvious class bias into the practice of alternative insemination. Far more high-tech, innovative, expensive, and therefore, uncommon, is a procreative strategy some lesbian couples now are adopting in which an ovum is extracted from one woman, fertilized with donor sperm, and then implanted in her lover's uterus. The practical and legal consequences of this still "nascent" practice have not yet been tested, but the irony of deploying technology to assert a biological, and thereby a legal, social and emotional claim to maternal and family status throws the contemporary instability of all the relevant categories—biology, technology, nature, culture, maternity, family— into bold relief.

While the advent of AIDS inhibited joint procreative ventures between lesbians and gay men, the epidemic also fostered stronger social and political solidarity between the two populations and stimulated gay men to keener interest in forming families. Their ranks are smaller and newer than those of lesbian mothers, but by the late 1980s gay men were also visibly engaged in efforts to become parents, despite far more limited opportunities to do so. Notwithstanding Arnold Schwarzenegger's 1994 celluloid pregnancy in *Junior* to the contrary,[18] not only do men still lack the biological capacity to derive personal benefits from most alternative reproductive technologies, but social prejudice also severely restricts gay male access to children placed for adoption, or even into foster care. Ever since Anita Bryant led a "Save the Children" campaign against gay rights in 1977, right-wing mobilizations in diverse states, including Florida, New Hampshire, and Massachusetts, have successfully cast gay men, in particular, as threats to children and families and denied them the right to adopt or foster the young. Wishful gay fathers have persevered against these odds, resorting to private adoption and surrogacy arrangements, accepting the most difficult-to-place adoptees and foster children, or entering into shared social parenting arrangements with lesbian couples or single women.

Compelled to proceed outside conventional cultural and institutional channels, lesbian and gay male planned parenthood has become an increasingly complex, diverse, creative, and politicized, self-help enterprise. Because gays forge kin ties without established legal protections or norms, relationships between gay parents and their children suffer heightened legal and social risks. If the shock troops of gay parenthood were the formerly married individuals who battled for child custody during the 1970s, by the mid-1980s many lesbians and gays were shocked to find themselves battling each other, as custody conflicts between lesbian co-parents or between lesbian parents and sperm donors and/or other relatives began to reach the dockets and to profoundly challenge the judicial doctrinal resources of family courts.[19] Despite a putative "best interests of the child" standard, "normal" heterosexual family prejudices instead guided virtually all the judges who heard these early cases. Biological claims of kinship nearly always trumped those of social parenting, even in heart-rending circumstances of custody challenges to bereaved lesbian "widows" who, with their deceased lovers, had jointly planned for, reared, loved and supported children since their birth.[20] Likewise, judges routinely honored fathers' rights arguments by favoring parental claims of donors who had contributed nothing more than sperm to their offspring over those of lesbians who had co-parented from the outset, *even when these men had expressly agreed to abdicate paternal rights or responsibilities.* The first, and still rare, exception to this rule involved a donor who did not bring his paternity suit until the child was ten years old.[21] And while numerous sperm donors have reneged on their prenatal agreements, thus far no lesbian mother has sued a donor to attain parental terms different from those to which he first agreed. On the other hand, in the one case in which a lesbian biological mother has sought financial support from her former lesbian partner, a New York court found the non-biological co-parent to be a parent. Here, the state's fiduciary interest, rather than gay rights, governed the decision.[22]

Perhaps the most poignant paradox in gay and lesbian family history concerns the quiet heroism displayed by gays compelled to struggle for family status precisely when forces mobilized in the name of The Family conspire to deny this to them. The widely publicized saga of the Sharon Kowalski case, in which the natal family of a lesbian who had been severely disabled in a car crash successfully opposed her guardianship by her chosen life-companion, proved particularly galvanizing in this cause, perhaps because all of the contestants were adults. After eight years of legal and political struggle, Sharon's lover, Karen Thompson, finally won a reversal, in a belated, but highly visible, landmark victory for gay family rights.[23]

Gay family struggles have achieved other significant victories, like the 1989 *Braschi* decision by New York state's top court, which granted a gay man protection against eviction from his deceased lover's rent-controlled apartment by explicitly defining family in inclusive, social terms:

> the exclusivity and longevity of the relationship, the level of emotional and financial commitment, the manner in which the parties have conducted their everyday lives and held themselves out to society, and the reliance placed upon one another for daily family services . . . it is the totality of the relationship as evidenced by the dedication, caring, and self-sacrifice of the parties which should, in the final analysis, control.[24]

Currently, one of the most active fronts in the gay family rights campaign is the struggle for second-parent adoption rights, which enable a lesbian or gay man to adopt a lover's children without removing the legal parent's custody rights. Numerous lesbian couples (including former undersecretary of Housing and Urban Development and 1995 San Francisco mayoral candidate, Roberta Achtenberg, and her partner) as well as a handful of gay male couples, have won this form of legal parenthood, which has been granted at the state court level in Vermont, Massachusetts, and New York, and at local levels in several additional states. Curiously, this particular struggle is more advanced in the United States than in Canada,

Europe, or even in the Nordic countries whose legislatures explicitly excluded adoption rights when they legalized a form of gay marriage.[25] Probably the decentralized character of family law in the U.S. accounts for this anomaly.

Of course, even in the United States, very few jurisdictions grant second-parent adoptions, which, in any case, provide only a second-class route to parenthood for lesbian or gay co-parents, because it requires a home study conducted after a child is born. No jurisdiction allows gay couples to legally parent a child together from its birth.[26] Moreover, the highly politicized character of family change in the United States renders even this second-class option painfully vulnerable to unfavorable political winds. For example, during his unsuccessful bid for the 1996 Republican presidential nomination, California's Governor Pete Wilson courted his party's right wing, profamily factions by reimposing state barriers to lesbian and gay, second-parent adoptions that had recently been dismantled. The National Center for Lesbian Rights considers this right to be so crucial to the lesbian "profamily" cause that it revoked its former policy of abstaining from legal conflicts between lesbians over this issue. Convinced that the long-term, best interests of gay and lesbian parents and their children depend upon defining parenthood in social, rather than biological, terms, the Center decided to represent lesbian parents who are denied custody of their jointly reared children when their former lovers exploit the biological and homophobic prejudices of the judiciary.[27]

Here again, gay family politics telescope, rather than stray from, pervasive cultural trends. Gay second-parent adoptions, for example, trek a kin trail blazed by court responses to families reconstituted after divorce and remarriage. Courts first allowed some stepparents to adopt their new spouses' children without terminating the custody rights of the children's former parents. Gay family rights law bears a kind of second cousin tie to racial kin case law. Gay and lesbian custody victories rely heavily on a milestone race custody case, *Palmore* v. *Sidoti* (1984), which restored the custody rights of a divorced, white mother who lost her children after she married a black man. Even though *Palmore* was decided on strict legal principles governing race discrimination which do not yet apply to gender or sexual discrimination, several successful gay and lesbian custody decisions rely on its logic by refusing to interpret discrimination against their parents as serving "the best interests" of children. The first successful second-parent adoption award to a lesbian couple actually was a "third-parent" adoption on the model of stepparent adoption after divorce. The court granted co-parent status to the nonbiological mother without withdrawing it from the sperm donor father, a Native American, in order to honor the shared desires of all three parents to preserve the child's bicultural inheritance.[28]

As tabloid and talk show fare testify daily, culturally divisive struggles over babies secured or lost through alternative insemination, in vitro fertilization, ovum extraction, frozen embryos, surrogacy, transracial adoption, not to mention mundane processes of divorce and remarriage are not the special province of a fringe gay and lesbian minority. We now inhabit a world, however unwittingly, in which technology has up-ended the basic premises of the aged nature-nurture debate by rendering human biology more amenable to intervention than human society. Inevitably, therefore, contests between biological and social definitions of kinship, such as the notorious battles over "Baby M," involving surrogacy, and adopted baby Jessica DuBoer, will continue to proliferate and to rub social nerves raw. By their very existence, gay and lesbian families thwart potent cultural impulses to deny this unwelcome reality. Perhaps that is one source of the irrational hostility they elicit.

While one can discern a gradual political and judicial trend toward granting parental and family rights to gays, the legal situation in the 50 states remains starkly discriminatory, uneven, volatile, and replete with major setbacks for gay and lesbian parents, like the ongoing Sharon Bottoms case in Virginia in which a lesbian mother is fighting to regain custody of her young son.[29] The crucial, and chilling, fact remains that twenty-one states still criminalize sodomy with impunity, because in 1986 the U.S. Supreme Court in *Bowers* v. *Hardwick* upheld the constitutionality of this most basic impediment to civil rights or even survival for gay relationships. Gay and lesbian families certainly have come a long way since Stonewall, but a much longer road, studded with formidable stone walls, remains for them to traverse.

A More, or Less, Perfect Union?

Much nearer at hand, however, than most ever dared to imagine has come the momentous prospect of legal gay marriage. The idea of same-sex marriage used to draw nearly as many jeers from gays and lesbians as from nongays. As one lesbian couple recalls, "In 1981, we were a very, very small handful of lesbians who got married. We took a lot of flak from other lesbians, as well as heterosexuals. In 1981, we didn't know any other lesbians, not a single one, who had had a ceremony in Santa Cruz, and a lot of lesbians live in that city. Everybody was on our case about it. They said, What are you doing, How heterosexual. We really had to sell it."[30]

Less than a decade later, gay and lesbian couples could proudly announce their weddings and anniversaries, not only in the gay press, which now includes specialized magazines for gay and lesbian couples, like *Partners Magazine*, but even in such mainstream, Midwestern newspapers as the Minneapolis *Star Tribune*.[31] Jewish rabbis, Protestant ministers, Quaker meetings, and even some Catholic priests regularly perform gay and lesbian wedding or commitment ceremonies. This phenomenon is memorialized in cultural productions within the gay community, like "Chicks In White Satin," a documentary about a Jewish lesbian wedding which won prizes at recent gay film festivals, but it has also become a fashionable pop culture motif. In December 1995, the long-running TV sitcom program "Roseanne" featured a gay male wedding in a much-hyped episode called "December Bride." Even more provocative, however, was a prime-time lesbian wedding that aired one month later on

"Friends," the highest rated sitcom of the 1995–1996 television season. Making a cameo appearance on the January 18, 1996 episode, Candice Gingrich, the lesbian half-sister of right-wing Speaker of the House Newt Gingrich, conducted a wedding ceremony which joined the characters who play a lesbian couple on the series "in holy matrimony" and pronounced them "wife and wife."

When the very first social science research collection about gay parents was published in 1987, not even one decade ago, its editor concluded that however desirable such unions might be, "it is highly unlikely that marriages between same-sex individuals will be legalized in any state in the foreseeable future."[32] Yet, almost immediately thereafter, precisely this specter began to exercise imaginations across the political spectrum. A national poll reported by the *San Francisco Examiner* in 1989 found that 86 percent of lesbians and gay men supported legalizing same-sex marriage.[33] However, it is the pending *Baehr* v. *Lewin* court decision concerning same-sex marriage rights in Hawaii that has thrust this issue into escalating levels of front-page and prime-time prominence. Amidst rampant rumors that thousands of mainland gay and lesbian couples were stocking their hope chests with Hawaiian excursion fares, poised to fly to tropical altars the instant the first gay matrimonial bans falter, right-wing Christian groups began actively mobilizing resistance. Militant antiabortion leader Randall Terry of Operation Rescue flew to Hawaii in February 1996 to fight "queer marriage," and right-wing Christian women's leader and radio broadcast personality Beverly LaHaye urged her "Godly" listeners to fight gay marriage in Hawaii.[34]

Meanwhile, fearing that Hawaii will become a gay marriage mecca, state legislators have rushed to introduce bills that exclude same-sex marriages performed in other states from being recognized in their own, because the "full faith and credit" clause of the U.S. Constitution obligates interstate recognition of legal marriages. While fourteen states had rejected such bills by May 1995, eight others had passed them, and contests were underway in numerous others, including California.[35] On May 8, 1996, gay marriage galloped onto the nation's center political stage when Republicans introduced the Defense of Marriage Act (DOMA) which defines marriage in exclusively heterosexual terms, as "a legal union between one man and one woman as husband and wife."[36] The last legislation that Republican presidential candidate Bob Dole co-sponsored before he resigned from the Senate to pursue his White House bid full throttle, DOMA exploits homophobia to defeat President Clinton and the Democrats in November 1996. With Clinton severely bruised by the political debacle incited by his support for gay rights in the military when he first took office, but still dependent upon the support of his gay constituency, the President indeed found himself "wedged" between a rock and a very hard place. Unsurprisingly, he tried to waffle. Naming this a "time when we need to do things to strengthen the American family," Clinton publicly opposed same-sex marriage at the same time that he tried to reaffirm support for gay rights and to expose the divisive Republican strategy.[37]

Polemics favoring and opposing gay marriage rights now proliferate in editorial pages and legislatures across the nation, and mainstream religious bodies find themselves compelled to confront the issue. In March 1996 the Vatican felt called upon not merely to condemn same-sex marriage as a "moral disorder," but also to warn Catholics that they would themselves risk "moral censure" if they were to support "the election of the candidate who has formally promised to translate into law the homosexual demand."[38] Just one day after the Vatican published this admonition, the Central Conference of American Rabbis, which represents the large, generally liberal wing of Judaism, took a momentous action in direct opposition. The Conference resoundingly endorsed a resolution to "support the right of gay and lesbian couples to share fully and equally in the rights of civil marriage." Unsurprisingly, Orthodox rabbis immediately condemned the action as prohibited in the Bible and "another breakdown in the family unit."[39] One week later, in another historic development, a lead editorial in the *New York Times* strongly endorsed gay marriage.[40]

As with child custody, the campaign for gay marriage clings to legal footholds carved by racial justice pioneers. It is startling to recall how recent it was that the Supreme Court finally struck down anti-miscegenation laws. Not until 1967, that is only two years before Stonewall, did the high court, in Loving vs. Virginia, find state restrictions on interracial marriages to be unconstitutional. (Twenty states still had such restrictions on the books in 1967, only one state fewer than the twenty-one which currently prohibit sodomy.) A handful of gay couples quickly sought to marry in the 1970s through appeals to this precedent, but until three lesbian and gay male couples sued Hawaii in *Baehr* v. *Lewin* for equal rights to choose marriage partners without restrictions on gender, all U.S. courts had dismissed the analogy. In a historic ruling in 1993, the Hawaiian state Supreme Court remanded this suit to the state, requiring it to demonstrate a "compelling state interest" in prohibiting same-sex marriage, a strict scrutiny standard that few believe the state will be able to meet. Significantly, the case was neither argued nor adjudicated as a gay rights issue. Rather, just as ERA opponents once had warned and advocates had denied, passage of an equal rights amendment to Hawaii's state constitution in 1972 paved the legal foundation for *Baehr*.[41]

Most gay activists and legal scholars anticipate a victory for gay marriage when *Baehr* is finally decided early in 1997, but they do not all look forward to this prospect with great delight. Although most of their constituents desire the right to marry, gay activists and theorists continue to vigorously debate the politics and effects of this campaign. Refining earlier feminist and socialist critiques of the gender and class inequities of marriage, an articulate, vocal minority seeks not to extend the right to marry, but to dismantle an institution they regard as inherently, and irredeemably, hierarchical, unequal, conservative, and repressive. Nancy Polikoff, one of the most articulate lesbian legal activist-scholars opposed to the marriage campaign, argues that

Advocating lesbian and gay marriage will detract from, and even con-
tradict, efforts to unhook economic benefits from marriage and make
basic health care and other necessities available to all. It will also
require a rhetorical strategy that emphasizes similarities between our
relationships and heterosexual marriages, values long-term monogamous coupling above all other relationships, and denies the potential of
lesbian and gay marriage to transform the gendered nature of marriage
for all people. I fear that the very process of employing that rhetorical
strategy for the years it will take to achieve its objective will lead our
movement's public representatives, and the countless lesbians and gay
men who hear us, to believe exactly what we say.[42]

A second perspective supports legal marriage as one long-term
goal of the gay rights movement, but voices serious strategic objec-
tions to making this a priority before there is sufficient public support
to sustain a favorable ruling in Hawaii or the nation. Such critics fear
that a premature victory will prove pyrrhic, because efforts to defend
it against the vehement backlash it has already begun to incite are apt
to fail, after sapping resources and time better devoted to other urgent struggles for gay rights. Rather than risk a major setback for the
gay movement, they advise an incremental approach to establishing
legal family status for gay and lesbian kin ties through a multifaceted
struggle for family diversity.[43]

However, the largest, and most diverse, contingent of gay activist
voices now supports the marriage rights campaign, perhaps because
gay marriage can be read to harmonize with virtually every hue on
the gay ideological spectrum. Pro-gay marriage arguments range from
profoundly conservative to liberal humanist to radical and decon-
structive. Conservatives, like those radicals who still oppose marriage,
view it as an institution that promotes monogamy, commitment and
social stability, along with interests in private property, social conformity and mainstream values. They likewise agree that legalizing gay
marriage would further marginalize sexual radicals by segregating
counter-cultural gays and lesbians from the "whitebread" gay couples who could then choose to marry their way into Middle America.

Radicals and conservatives, in other words, envision the same prospect, but regard it with inverse sentiments.[44]

Liberal gays support legal marriage, of course, not only to affirm the legitimacy of their relationships and help sustain them in a hostile world, but as a straightforward matter of equal civil rights. As one long-coupled gay man expresses it: "I resent the fact that married people get lower taxes. But as long as there is this institution of marriage and heterosexuals have that privilege, then gay people should be able to do it too."[45] Liberals also recognize that marriage rights provide access to the social advantages of divorce law. "I used to say, 'Why do we want to get married? It doesn't work for straight people,' one gay lawyer comments. "But now I say we should care: They have the privilege of divorce and we don't. We're left out there to twirl around in pain."[46]

Less obvious or familiar, however, are cogent arguments in favor of gay marriage that some feminist and other critical gay legal theorists have developed in response to opposition within the gay community. Nan Hunter, for example, rejects feminist legal colleague Nancy Polikoff's belief that marriage is an unalterably sexist and heterosexist institution. Building upon critical theories that reject the notion that social institutions or categories have inherent, fixed meanings apart from their social contexts, Hunter argues that legalized same-sex marriage would have "enormous potential to destabilize the gendered definition of marriage for everyone."[47]

Evan Wolfson, director of the Marriage Project of the gay legal rights organization Lambda Legal Defense, who has submitted a brief in support of *Baehr*, pursues the logic of "anti-essentialism" even more consistently. The institution of marriage is neither inherently equal nor unequal, he argues, but depends upon an ever-changing cultural and political context.[48] (Anyone who doubts this need only consider such examples as polygamy, arranged marriages, or the same-sex unions in early Western history documented by the late Princeton historian, John Boswell.) Hoping to use marriage precisely to change its context, gay philosopher Richard Mohr argues that access to legal marriage would provide an opportunity to reconstruct its meaning by serving "as a nurturing ground for social marriage, and not (as now) as that which legally defines and creates marriage and so precludes legal examination of it." For Mohr, social marriage represents "the fused intersection of love's sanctity and necessity's demands," and does not necessarily depend upon sexual monogamy.[49]

Support for gay marriage, not long ago anathema to radicals and conservatives, gays and nongays, alike, now issues forth from ethical and political perspectives as diverse, and even incompatible, as these. The cultural and political context has changed so dramatically since Stonewall that it now seems easier to understand why marriage has come to enjoy overwhelming support in the gay community than to grasp the depth of resistance to the institution that characterized the early movement. Still, I take seriously many of the strategic concerns about the costly political risks posed by a premature campaign. Although surveys and electoral struggles suggest a gradual growth in public support for gay rights, that support is tepid, uneven and fickle, as the debacle over Clinton's attempt to combat legal exclusion of gays from the military made distressingly clear. Thus, while 52 percent of those surveyed in a 1994 *Time* magazine/CNN poll claimed to consider gay lifestyle acceptable, 64 percent did not want to legalize gay marriages or to permit gay couples to adopt children.[50]

Gay marriage, despite its apparent compatibility with mainstream family values sentiment, raises far more threatening questions than does military service about gender relations, sexuality and family life. Few contemporary politicians, irrespective of their personal convictions, display the courage to confront this contradiction, even when urged to do so by gay conservatives. In *Virtually Normal: An Argument About Homosexuality*, *New Republic* editor Andrew Sullivan develops the "conservative case for gay marriage," that he earlier published as an op-ed, which stresses the contribution gay marriage could make to a conservative agenda for family and political life. A review of Sullivan's book in the *New Yorker* points out that, "here is where the advocates of gay rights can steal the conservatives' clothes."[51] The epigraph to this chapter by Jonathan Rauch about the insignificance of the homosexual minority comes from a *Wall Street Journal* op-ed he wrote to persuade Republicans that they should support legal gay marriage, not only because it is consistent with conservative values, but to guard against the possibility that gay rights advocates will exploit the party's inconsistency on this issue to political advantage.[52]

The logic behind the conservative case for gay marriage strikes me as compelling. Most importantly, gay marriage would strengthen the ranks of those endangered two-parent, "intact," married-couples families whose praises conservative, "profamily" enthusiasts never seem to tire of singing. Unsurprisingly, however, the case has won few nongay conservative converts to the cause. After all, homophobia is a matter of passion and politics, not logic. The religious right regards homosexuality as an abomination, and it has effectively consolidated its influence over the Republican Party. For example, in 1994, Republicans in the Montana state senate went so far as to pass a bill that would require anyone convicted of homosexual acts to register for life as a violent offender. They reversed their vote in response to an outpouring of public outrage.[53] It was not long afterward, however, that Republican presidential contender Robert Dole returned the thousand-dollar campaign contribution from the gay Log Cabin Republicans in the name, of course, of family values. Nor have figures prominent in the centrist, secular neo-family-values campaign or the communitarian movement, whose professed values affirm both communal support for marital commitment and for tolerance, displayed much concern for such consistency.[54] And even when, in the 1995 fall preelection season, President Clinton sought to "shore up" his standing among gays and lesbians by announcing his administration's support of a bill to outlaw employment discrimination against gays, he specifically withheld his support from gay marriage.[55] First Lady Hillary Rodham Clinton's recent book, *It Takes a Village*, ostensibly written to challenge "false nostalgia for family values," fails even to mention gay marriage or gay families, let alone to advocate village rights and resources for children whose parents are gay.[56]

Despite my personal political baptism in the heady, anti-family crucible of early second wave feminism, I, for one, have converted to the long-term cause. A "postmodern" ideological stew of discordant convictions enticed me to this table. Like Wolfson, Mohr, and Hunter, I have come to believe that legitimizing gay and lesbian marriages would promote a democratic, pluralistic expansion of the meaning, practice, and politics of family life in the United States. This could help to supplant the destructive sanctity of *the family* with respect for diverse and vibrant *families*.

To begin with, the liberal implications of legal gay marriage are far from trivial, as the current rush by the states and Congress to nullify them should confirm. The Supreme Court is certain to have its docket flooded far into the next century with constitutional conflicts that a favorable decision in Hawaii, or elsewhere, will unleash. Under the "full faith and credit" provision of the Constitution, which requires the 50 states to recognize each other's laws, legal gay marriage in one state could begin to threaten anti-sodomy laws in all the others. Policing marital sex would be difficult to legitimate, and differential prosecution of conjugal sex among same-sex couples could violate equal protection legislation. Likewise, if gay marriages were legalized, the myriad state barriers to child custody, adoption, fertility services, inheritance, and other family rights that lesbians and gay men currently suffer could also become subject to legal challenge. Moreover, it seems hard to overestimate the profound cultural implications for the struggle against the pernicious effects of legally condoned homophobia that would ensue were lesbian and gay relationships to be admitted into the ranks of legitimate kinship. In a society that forbids most public school teachers and counselors even the merest expression of tolerance for homosexuality, while lesbian and gay youth attempt suicide at rates three to five times greater than other youth,[57] granting full recognition to even just whitebread lesbian and gay relationships could have dramatic, and salutary, consequences.

Of course, considerations truer to some of my earlier, more visionary feminist convictions also invite me to join the gay wedding procession. For while I share some of Polikoff's disbelief that same-sex marriage can in itself dismantle the patterned gender and sexual injustices of the institution, I do believe it could make a potent contribution to those projects, as the research on gay relationships I discuss below seems to indicate. Moreover, as Mohr suggests, admitting gays to the wedding banquet invites gays and nongays alike to consider the kinds of place settings that could best accommodate the diverse needs of all contemporary families.

Subjecting the conjugal institution to this sort of heightened democratic scrutiny could help it to assume varied creative forms. If we begin to value the meaning and quality of intimate bonds over their customary forms, there are few limits to the kinds of marriage and kinship patterns people might wish to devise. The "companionate marriage," a much celebrated, but less often realized, ideal of modern sociological lore, could take on new life. Two friends might decide to marry without basing their bond on erotic or romantic attachment, as Dorthe, a prominent Danish lesbian activist who had initially opposed the campaign for gay marriage, fantasized after her nation's parliament approved gay registered partnerships: "If I am going to marry it will be with one of my oldest friends in order to share pensions and things like that. But I'd never marry a lover. That is the advantage of being married to a close friend. Then, you never have to marry a lover!"[58] Or, more radical still, perhaps some might dare to question the dyadic limitations of Western marriage and seek some of the benefits of extended family life through small-group marriages arranged to share resources, nurturance and labor. After all, if it is true that "The Two-Parent Family Is Better"[59] than a single-parent family, as family-values crusaders like David Popenoe tirelessly proclaim, might not three-, four-, or more-parent families be better yet, as many utopian communards have long believed?

While conservative advocates of gay marriage surely would balk at such radical visions, they correctly realize that putative champions of committed relationships and of two-parent families who oppose gay marriage can be charged with gross hypocrisy on this score. For access to legal marriage not only would promote long-term, committed intimacy among gay couples, but also would afford invaluable protection to the children of gay parents, as well as indirect protection to closeted gay youth who reside with nongay parents. Clearly, only through a process of massive denial of the fact that millions of children living in gay and lesbian families are here, and here to stay, can anyone genuinely concerned with the best interests of children deny their parents the right to marry.

In the face of arguments for legalizing gay marriage as compelling and incongruent as these, it is hard to dispute Evan Wolfson's enthusiastic claim that, "The brilliance of our movement's taking on marriage is that marriage is, at once and truly, both conservative and transformative, easily understood in basic human terms of equality and respect, and liberating in its individual and social potential."[60]

In the Best Interests of Whose Children?

The most cursory survey of the existing empirical research on gay and lesbian families reveals the depth of sanctioned discrimination such families continue to suffer and the absence of evidence to justify this iniquity. To be sure, substantial limitations mar the social science research on this subject, which is barely past its infancy. For openers, mainstream journals, even those specializing in family research, warmed to this subject startlingly late and little, relegating the domain primarily to sexologists, clinicians and a handful of movement scholars and their sympathizers and opponents. A recent survey of the three leading journals of family research in the United States found only 12 of the 2,598 articles published between 1980 and 1993—less than .05 percent—focused on the families of lesbians and gay men, which, even by conservative estimates, make up at least 5 percent of U.S. families.[61] The research that does exist, however, has deficiencies that skew results so as to exaggerate, rather than understate, any defects of gay and lesbian families. Until very recently, most investigators began with a deviance perspective, seeking, whether homophobically or defensively, to test the validity of the popular prejudice that gay parenting is harmful to children. In other words, the reigning premise has been that gay and lesbian families are dangerously, and *prima facie*, "queer" in the pejorative sense, unless proven otherwise. Taking children reared by nongay parents as the unquestioned norm, most studies asymmetrically ask whether lesbian and gay parents hinder their children's emotional, cognitive, gender, and sexual development. Because lesbian and gay planned parenthood is so new, and its progeny so young, nearly all of the studies to date sample the ranks of formerly married parents who had children before they divorced and came out of the closet. The studies are generally small-scale and draw disproportionately from urban, white, middle-class populations. Frequently they make misleading comparisons between divorced lesbian and nongay, single-mother households by ignoring the presence or absence of lesbian life partners or other caretakers in the former.[62]

Despite such limitations, psychologists, social psychologists, and sociologists have by now conducted dozens of studies which provide overwhelming support for the "proven otherwise" thesis. Almost without exception they conclude, albeit in defensive or patronizing tones, that lesbian and gay parents do not produce inferior, or even particularly different kinds of children than do other parents. Studies generally find no significant differences in school achievement, social adjustment, mental health, gender identity, or sexual orientation between the two groups of children. As Joan Laird's overview of research on lesbian and gay parents summarizes:

> a generation of research has failed to demonstrate that gays or lesbians are any less fit to parent than their heterosexual counterparts. Further-

more, a substantial number of studies on the psychological and social development of children of lesbian and gay parents have failed to produce any evidence that children of lesbian or gay parents are harmed or compromised or even differ from, in any significant ways along a host of psychosocial developmental measures, children raised in heterosexual families.[63]

Research to date finds lesbian and gay parents to be at least as effective, nurturant, responsible, loving and loved, as other parents. The rare small differences reported tend to favor gay parents, portraying them as somewhat more nurturant and tolerant, and their children, in turn, more tolerant and empathic, and less aggressive than those reared by nongay parents.[64] In April 1995, British researchers published the results of their unusual sixteen-year-long study which followed 25 children brought up by lesbian mothers and 21 brought up by heterosexual mothers from youth to adulthood. They found that the young adults raised in lesbian households had better relationships with their mothers' lesbian partners than the young adults brought up by heterosexual single mothers had with their mothers' male partners.[65] Published research to date seems to vindicate one ten-year-old girl who, rather apologetically, deems herself privileged to be the daughter of two lesbian parents: "But I think you get more love with two moms. I know other kids have a mom and a dad, but I think that moms give more love than dads. This may not be true, but it's what I think." Her opinion is shared by a six-year-old girl from another lesbian family: "I don't tell other kids at school about my mothers because I think they would be jealous of me. Two mothers is better than one."[66]

In light of the inhospitable, often outrightly hostile climate which gay families, by their very existence, encounter, this seems a remarkable achievement. One sign that mainstream social scientists are beginning to recognize the achievement is the inclusion of Laird's chapter on "Lesbian and Gay Families" in the 1993 edition of a compendium of research, *Normal Family Processes*, whose first edi-

tion in 1982 ignored the subject.[67] Researchers have begu̅
and to initiate, a mature, creative, undefensive approach to̅
the full range of gay and lesbian families. Coming to terms wi̅
realities of the postmodern family condition, such studies begin w̅
a pluralistic premise concerning the legitimacy and dignity of diverse
family structures. They ask whether and how gay and lesbian families
differ, rather than deviate, from nongay families; they attend as much
to the differences among such families as to those dividing them
from nongays; and they explore the particular benefits as well as the
burdens such families bestow on their members.[68]

I am confident that this kind of research will discover more
advantages of gay and lesbian family life for participants and "the rest
of us" than have yet been explored. Most obvious, certainly, are
mental-health rewards for gay and lesbian youth fortunate enough to
come of age in such families. Currently most youth who experience
homosexual inclinations either conceal their desires from their immediate kin or risk serious forms of rejection. State hostility to gay
parents can have tragic results. In 1994, for example, the Nebraska
Department of Social Services adopted a policy forbidding lesbian or
gay foster homes, and the next day a seventeen-year-old openly gay
foster child committed suicide, because he feared he would be re-
moved from the supportive home of his gay foster parents.[69]

Of course, this speaks precisely to the heart of what homophobes
most fear, that public acceptance of lesbian and gay families will
spawn an epidemic of gay youth. As Pat Robertson so crudely explained to a Florida audience, "That gang of idiots running the
ACLU, The National Education Association, the National Organization of Women, they don't want religious principles in our schools.
Instead of teaching the Ten Commandments, they want to teach kids
how to be homosexuals."[70] Attempting to respond to such anxieties,
most defenders of gay families to date have stressed the irrelevance of
parental sexual identity to that of their children. Sympathetic researchers repeatedly, and in my view wrongheadedly, maintain that
lesbian and gay parents are no more likely than nongay parents to

:n. Laird, for example, laments: "One of
; that children of gay parents will them-
: that daughters will be more masculine
ian "normal" children. A number of re-
hat the sexual orientations/preferences of
parents do not differ from those whose
parents are heterosexual.

I find this claim illogical, unlikely and unwittingly anti-gay. Ironically, it presumes the very sort of fixed, "essentialist" definition of
sexuality that the best contemporary gay and lesbian scholarship has
challenged. Although it is clearly true that, until now, nearly all
homosexuals, like almost everyone else, have been reared by nongays, it is equally clear that sexual desire and identity do not represent
a singular fixed trait that expresses itself free of cultural context.
However irresolvable eternal feuds over the relative weight of nature
and nurture may forever prove to be, historical and anthropological
data leave no doubt that culture profoundly influences sexual meanings and practices.[72] Homophobes are quite correct to believe that
environmental conditions incite or inhibit expressions of same-sex
desire, no matter its primary source. If culture had no influence on
sexual identity, there would not have emerged the movement for gay
and lesbian family rights that inspired me to write this chapter.

Contrary to what most current researchers claim, public acceptance of gay and lesbian families should, in fact, slightly expand the
percentage of youth who would dare to explore their same-sex desires. In fact, a careful reading of the studies does suggest just this.
Children reared by lesbian or gay parents feel greater openness to gay
or bisexuality. In January 1996, the researchers who conducted the
long-term British study conceded this point, after issuing the obligatory reassurance that, "the commonly held assumption that children brought up by lesbian mothers will themselves grow up to be
lesbian or gay is not supported by the findings." Two of the 25 young
adults in the study who were reared by lesbians themselves grew up
to identify as lesbians, but none of the 21 who were reared in the

comparison group of heterosexual mothers identify as lesbian or gay. More pertinent, in my view, five daughters and one son of lesbian mothers, but none of the children of heterosexual mothers, reported having had a same-sex erotic experience of some sort, prompting the researchers to acknowledge that, "It seems that growing up in an accepting atmosphere enables individuals who are attracted to same-sex partners to pursue these relationships."[73] This prospect should disturb only those whose antipathy to homosexuality derives from deeply held religious convictions or irrational prejudice.

The rest of us could benefit from permission to explore and develop sexually free from the rigid prescriptions of what Adrienne Rich memorably termed "compulsory heterosexuality."[74] Currently, lesbian and gay parents grant their children such permission much more generously than do other parents. Not only do they tend to be less doctrinaire or phobic about sexual diversity than heterosexual parents, but, wishing to spare their children the burdens of stigma, some gay parents actually prefer that their youngsters do not become gay. Indeed, despite the ubiquity of Pat Robertson's sort of alarmist, propagandistic warnings, "advice on how to help your kids turn out gay," as cultural critic Eve Sedgwick sardonically puts it, "is less ubiquitous than you might think."[75]

Heterosexual indoctrination is far more pervasive and far the greater danger. Contemporary adolescent culture is even more mercilessly homophobic, or perhaps less hypocritically so, than most mainstream adult prejudices countenance. Verbal harassment, ridicule, hazing, and ostracism of "faggots," "bull-dykes," and "queers" —quotidien features of our popular culture—are particularly blatant among teens. "Sometimes I feel like no one really knows what I'm going through," one fifteen-year-old daughter of a lesbian laments: "Don't get me wrong. I really do love my mom and all her friends, but being gay is just not acceptable to other people. Like at school, people make jokes about dykes and fags, and it really bothers me. I mean I bite my tongue, because if I say anything, they wonder, Why is she sticking up for them?"[76] In a recent survey, nearly half the teen victims of reported violent physical assaults identified their sexual orientation as a precipitating factor. Tragically, family members inflicted 61 percent of these assaults on gay youth.[77]

Little wonder such disproportionate numbers of gay youth commit suicide. Studies attribute one-third of teen suicide attempts to gay youth.[78] To evade harassment, most of the survivors suffer their clandestine difference in silent isolation, often at great cost to their esteem, social relationships and to their very experience of adolescence itself. One gay man bought his life partner a Father's Day card, because he, "realized that in a lot of ways we've been brother and father to each other since we've had to grow up as adults. Because of homophobia, gay people don't have the same opportunity as heterosexuals to be ourselves when we are teenagers. A lot of times you have to postpone the experiences until you're older, until you come out."[79]

The increased social visibility and community building of gays and lesbians has vastly improved the quality of life for most gay adults. Ironically, however, Linnea Due, author of a recent book about growing up gay in the '90s, was disappointed to find that the visible movement has had contradictory consequences for gay teens. Due expected to find conditions much better for gay youth than when she grew up in the silent '60s. Instead, many teens thought their circumstances had become more difficult, because, as one young man put it, "Now they know we're here."[80]

While most youth with same-sex desires will continue to come of age closeted in nongay families into the forseeable future, they would surely gain some emotional comfort from greater public acceptance of gay and lesbian families. Yet in 1992 when the New York City board of education tried to introduce the Rainbow multicultural curriculum guide, which advocated respect for lesbian and gay families in an effort "to help increase the tolerance and acceptance of the lesbian/gay community and to decrease the staggering number of hate crimes perpetrated against them," public opposition became so vehement that it contributed to the dismissal of Schools Chancellor Joseph Fernandez.[81]

Indeed, the major documented special difficulties that children in gay families experience derive directly from legal discrimination and social prejudice. As one otherwise well-adjusted, sixteen-year-old son of a lesbian puts it: "If I came out and said my mom was gay, I'd be treated like an alien."[82] Children of gay parents are vicarious victims of rampant homophobia and institutionalized heterosexism. They suffer all of the considerable economic, legal and social disadvantages imposed on their parents, sometimes even more harshly. They risk losing a beloved parent or co-parent at the whim of a judge. They can be denied access to friends by the parents of playmates. Living in families that are culturally invisible or despised, the children suffer ostracism by proxy, forced continually to negotiate conflicts between loyalty to home, mainstream authorities and peers.

However, as the Supreme Court belatedly concluded in 1984, when it repudiated discrimination against interracial families in *Palmore* v. *Sidoti*, and as should be plain good sense, the fact that children of stigmatized parents bear an unfair burden provides no critique of their families, and the social cloud that confronts them has its silver lining. The sad *social* fact of prejudice and discrimination indicts the family values of the bigoted society, not the stigmatized family. In the words of the Court: "private biases may be outside the reach of the law, but the law cannot, directly or indirectly, give them effect."[83] Although the strict scrutiny standards that now govern race discrimination do not apply to sexual orientation discrimination, several courts in recent years have relied on the logic of Palmore in gay custody cases. These decisions have approved lesbian and gay custody awards while explicitly acknowledging that community disapproval of their parents' sexual identity would require "greater than ordinary fortitude" from the children, but that in return they might more readily learn that, "people of integrity do not shrink from bigots." A New Jersey appellate court enumerated potential benefits children might derive from being raised by lesbian or gay parents that could serve as child-rearing ideals for a democracy: "emerge better equipped to search out their own standards of right and wrong, better able to perceive that the majority is not always correct in its moral judgments, and better able to understand the importance of conforming their beliefs to the requirements of reason and tested knowledge, not the constraints of currently popular sentiment or prejudice."[84] The testimony of one fifteen-year-old daughter of a lesbian mother and gay father indicates just this sort of outcome: "I think I am more open-minded than if I had straight parents. Sometimes kids at school make a big deal out of being gay. They say it's stupid and stuff like that. But they don't really know, because they are not around it. I don't say anything to them, but I know they are wrong. I get kind of mad, because they don't know what they are talking about."[85]

In fact, literature suggests that parents and children alike who live in fully closeted lesbian and gay families tend to suffer more than members of "out" gay families who contend with stigma directly.[86] Of course, gay parents who shroud their families in closets do so for compelling cause. Many judges make the closet an explicit condition for awarding custody or visitation rights to gay or lesbian parents, at times imposing direct restrictions on the parents' participation in gay social or political activity.[87] Or, fearing judicial homophobia, some parents live in mortal terror of losing their children, like one divorced lesbian in Kansas City whose former, violent husband has threatened an ugly custody battle if anyone finds out about her lesbianism.[88] Should not the special burdens of the closet that gay families bear indict the "don't ask, don't tell" values of a society that treats gay families like cultural skeletons rather than those of the families denied the light and air of social respect?

Heroically, more and more brave new "queer" families are refusing the clandestine life. If a recent, comprehensive, survey article, "The Families of Lesbians and Gay Men: A New Frontier in Family Research,"[89] is correctly titled, then research on fully planned lesbian and gay families is its vanguard outpost. Researchers estimated that by 1990, between five and ten thousand lesbians in the United States had given birth to chosen children,[90] and the trend has increased visibly in the 1990s. Although this represents a small fraction of the biological and adopted children who live with lesbian parents, planned lesbian births, as Kath Weston suggests, "began to over-shadow these other kinds of dependents, assuming a symbolic sig-nificance for lesbians and gay men disproportionate to their numbers."[91] Lesbian "turkey-baster" babies are equally symbolic to those who abhor the practice. National Fatherhood Initiative orga-nizer David Blankenhorn, for example, calls for restricting sperm bank services to infertile married couples in order to inhibit the production of such "radically fatherless children," and similar con-cerns have been expressed in such popular publications as *U.S. News and World Report* and the *Atlantic* monthly.[92] (Interestingly, restric-tions that limit access to donor sperm exclusively to married women are widespread in Europe, even in the liberal Nordic nations.) Be-cause discrimination against prospective gay and lesbian adoptive parents leads most to conceal their sexual identity, it is impossible to estimate how many have succeeded in adopting or fostering chil-dren, but this too has become a visible form of gay planned parent-hood.[93]

Research on planned gay parenting is too young to be more than suggestive, but initial findings give more cause for gay pride than alarm. Parental relationships tend to be more cooperative and egal-itarian than among heterosexual parents, childrearing more nur-turant, children more affectionate.[94] On the other hand, lesbian mothers do bear some particular burdens. Like straight women who bear children through insemination, they confront the vexing ques-tion of how to negotiate their children's knowledge of and relation-ship to sperm donors. As Hollywood's 1994 romantic comedy *Made in America* spoofed, some progeny of unknown donors, like many adopted children, certainly do quest for contact with their genetic fathers. One ten-year-old girl conceived by private donor insemina-tion explains why she was relieved to find her biological father: "I wanted to find my dad because it was hard knowing I had a dad but not knowing who he was. It was like there was a missing piece."[95]

Lesbian couples planning a pregnancy contend with some unique questions and challenges concerning the relationship between biological and social maternity. They must decide which woman will try to become pregnant and how to negotiate feelings of jealousy, invisibility, and displacement that may be more likely to arise between the two than between a biological mother and father. Struggling to equalize maternal emotional stakes and claims, some lesbian couples decide to alternate the childbearing role, others attempt simultaneous pregnancies, and some, as we have seen, employ reproductive technology to divide the genetic and gestational components of procreation. Sometimes a nongestational lesbian mother jointly breastfeeds the baby her partner bears. Some of these lesbian mothers assume disproportionate responsibility for child care to compensate for their biological "disadvantage," and others give their surnames to their partner's offspring.

Planned lesbian and gay families, however, most fully realize the early Planned Parenthood goal, "every child a wanted child," as one twelve-year-old son of a lesbian recognized: "I think that if you are a child of a gay or lesbian, you have a better chance of having a great parent. If you are a lesbian, you have to go through a lot of trouble to get a child, so that child is really wanted."[96] Disproportionately "queer" families choose to reside in and construct communities that support family and social diversity. Partly because fertility and adoption services are expensive and often difficult to attain, intentional gay parents are disproportionately better educated and more mature than other parents. Preliminary research indicates that these advantages more than offset whatever problems their special burdens cause their children. Clearly, it is in the interest of all our children to afford their families social dignity and respect.

If we exploit the research with this aim in mind, deducing a rational wish list for public policy is quite a simple matter. A straightforward, liberal, equal rights agenda for lesbians and gays would seem the obvious and humane course. In the best interests of all children, we would provide lesbian and gay parents equal access to marriage, child custody, adoption, foster children, fertility services, inheritance, employment, and all social benefits. We would adopt "rainbow" curricula within our schools and our public media that promote the kind of tolerance and respect for family and sexual diversity that Laura Sebastian, an eighteen-year-old reared by her divorced mother and her mother's lesbian lover, advocates: "A happy child has happy parents, and gay people can be as happy as straight ones. It doesn't matter what kids have—fathers, mothers, or both— they just need love and support. It doesn't matter if you are raised by a pack of dogs, just as long as they love you! It's about time lesbians and gays can have children. It's everybody's right as a human be- ing."[97] We would expand support groups for gay youth and teen suicide prevention programs. In the name of our children, we would do all this and more, were there a rational relationship between empirical social science and public rhetoric and policy. Yet in a world so much the captive of virtual social science and virtual family values, how hopelessly utopian such an agenda appears!

If We Could Only Get Used to It

Far from esoteric, the experiences of diverse genres of gay and les- bian "families we choose" bear on many of the most feverishly con- tested issues in contemporary family politics. They can speak to our mounting cultural paranoia over whether fathers are expendable, to nature-nurture controversies over sexual and gender identities and the gender division of labor, to the meaning and purpose of voluntary marriage, and most broadly, to those ubiquitous family values con- tests over the relative importance for children of family structure or process, of biological or psychological parents.

From the African-American Million Man March in October 1995, the ecstatic mass rallies currently attended by hundreds of thousands of Christian male Promise Keepers, and Blankenhorn's National Fatherhood Initiative pledge campaign, to California gov- ernor Pete Wilson's 1996 state of the state address and President

Clinton's 1996 state of the union address, the nation seems to be gripped by cultural obsession over the decline of dependable dads. Of course, feminists like myself heartily welcome men's efforts to assume their full share of responsibility for the children they intentionally sire, as well as the ones they acquire.[98] After all, feminists spearheaded struggles coaxing fathers to share equally the drudgery and divinity of childrearing, at times with paradoxical costs to maternal self-interest.[99] This is quite a different matter, however, from nostalgic, reactionary moves to reify genetic paternity or stereotypical masculinity as crucial to the welfare of children and the nation alike.

Here is where research on lesbian families, particularly on planned lesbian couple families, could prove of no small import. Thus far, as we have seen, such research offers no brief for Blankenhorn's angst over "radically fatherless children," or does research on other types of families without fathers justify such paternalistic alarm. For example, a careful, comprehensive study of eighth-graders living in single-parent households found that boys derived no benefits from living with fathers rather than mothers: "of the 35 social psychological and educational outcomes studied, we cannot find even one in which both males and females benefit significantly from living with their same-sex parent."[100] Even more challenging to those who seem to believe that the mere presence of a father in a family confers significant benefits on his children are surprising data reported in a recent study of youth and violence conducted by Kaiser Permanente and Children Now. The study of 1,000 eleven- to seventeen-year-olds and of 150 seven- to ten-year-olds found that, contrary to popular belief, 68 percent of the "young people exposed to higher levels of health and safety threats" were from conventional two-parent families. Moreover, rather poignantly, fathers were among the last people that troubled teens would turn to for help, even when they lived in conventional two-parent families. Only 10 percent of the young people in such two-parent families said they would seek their father's advice first, compared with 44 percent who claimed they would turn first to their mothers, and 26 percent who would first seek help from friends. Many more youth were willing to discuss concerns over their health, safety, and sexuality with nurses or doctors.[101] Thus, empirical social science to date, like the historical record, gives us sound cause to regard either fathers or mothers alike as "expendable." It is the quality, commitment and character of parents, rather than their gender, that truly matter.

Similarly, research on the relationships of gay male and lesbian couples depicts diverse models for intimacy from which others could profit. "Freed" from normative conventions and institutions that govern heterosexual gender and family relationships, self-consciously "queer" couples and families, by necessity, have had to reflect much more seriously on the meaning and purpose of their intimate commitments. Studies that compare lesbian, gay male, and heterosexual couples find intriguing contrasts in their characteristic patterns of intimacy. Gender seems to shape domestic values and practices more powerfully than sexual identity, so that same-sex couples tend to be more compatible than heterosexual couples. For example, both lesbian and straight women seem to be more likely than either gay or straight men to value their relationships over their work. Yet both lesbian and gay male couples agree that both parties should be employed, while married men are less likely to agree with wives who wish to work. Predictably, same-sex couples share more interests and time together than married couples. Also unsurprising, lesbian couples tend to have the most egalitarian relationships, and married heterosexual couples the least. Lesbian and gay male couples both share household chores more equally and with less conflict than do married couples, but they share them differently. Lesbian couples tend to share most tasks while gay males more frequently assign tasks "to each according to his abilities," schedules, and preferences.[102]

Gender differences in sexuality are particularly striking and intriguing, because in this arena married women may be imposing more of their preferences on their husbands than conventional lore might predict. Gay male couples tend to have much more active, nonexclusive and casual sex lives than either lesbian or married couples. Nearly two-thirds of the gay male couples studied by sociologists Blumstein and Schwartz in 1983, before AIDS had reached visible epidemic proportions, practiced open relationships, but the clear majority of both lesbian and married couples were monogamous. While sexual frequency was lowest among lesbian couples, they considered themselves more compatible sexually than did either married couples or gay men. Husbands and wives disagreed the most about their sexual compatibility (with husbands claiming greater compatibility than wives reported), but gay men were the least troubled by sexual incompatibility, because they generally invested sex with fewer possessive, romantic or emotional meanings than did most women or married men.[103]

Each of these modal patterns for intimacy and sexuality has its particular strengths and vulnerabilities. Gender conventions and gender fluidity alike have advantages and limitations, as Blumstein and Schwartz and other researchers have discussed. For example, gay men who seek sexual monogamy can have as much trouble as do many heterosexual men who wish to escape its restrictions.[104] Getting used to queer families would not mean converting to any characteristic patterns of intimacy, but coming to terms with the collapse of a monolithic cultural regime governing our intimate bonds. It would mean embracing a genuinely pluralist understanding that there are diverse, valid ways to form and sustain these which could benefit us all. In the end, Jonathan Rauch may be right in one respect, after all. If we reserve the term homosexuality to signify the expression of same-sex desire, it should indeed be of little public concern. "The rest of us," however, share a great interest in becoming so used to the presence of gay and lesbian families among us that the very label will once again come to seem embarrassingly queer.

If there is anything truly distinctive about lesbian and gay families, it is how unambiguously the substance of their relationships takes precedence over their form, their emotional and social commitments over genetic claims. Compelled to exercise "good, old-fashioned American" ingenuity in order to fulfill familial desires, gays and lesbians improvisationally assemble a patchwork of blood and intentional relations—gay, straight and other—into creative, extended kin bonds.[105] Gay communities more adeptly integrate single individuals into their social worlds than does mainstream heterosexual society, a social skill quite valuable in a world in which divorce, widowhood and singlehood are increasingly normative. Because queer families must continually, self-consciously migrate in and out of the closet, they also hone bicultural skills particularly suitable for life in a multicultural society.[106] Self-identified queer families serve on the pioneer outpost of the postmodern family condition, confronting most directly its features of improvisation, ambiguity, diversity, contradiction, self-reflection and flux.

Even the distinctive, indeed the definitional, burden that pervasive homophobia imposes on lesbian and gay families does not fully distinguish them from other contemporary families. Unfortunately, prejudice, intolerance, and disrespect for "different" or "other" families is all too commonplace in the contemporary world, and it diminishes us all. Ethnocentric and intolerant familism harms the families of many immigrants, interracial couples, single mothers (be they unwed or divorced, impoverished or affluent) remarried couples, childless "yuppie" couples, bachelors and "spinsters," househusbands, and working mothers, the homeless, and it even places that vanishing, once-hallowed breed of full-time homemakers on the ("I'm just-a-housewife") defensive.

Gay and lesbian families simply brave intensified versions of widespread contemporary challenges. Both their plight and their pluck unequivocally expose the dangerous disjuncture between our family rhetoric and policy, on the one hand, and our family and social realities, on the other. Stubbornly denying the complex, pluralist array of contemporary families and kinship, most of our legal and social policies atavistically presume to serve a singular, "normal" family structure—the conventional, heterosexual, married-couple, nuclear family. In the name of children, politicians justify decisions that endanger them, and in the name of The Family, they cause grave harm to our families. It is time to get used to the postmodern family condition we all now inhabit. In the name of our families and democracy, we must move forward, not backward, to address the grave *social* threats that imperil us all.

Notes

·   ·   ·   ·   ·   ·   ·   ·   ·   ·

Sources for epigraphs are on page 170.

Introduction

1. The crime was committed in Illinois, and the quoted remarks by Illinois governor Edgar in the first epigraph were offered in defense of Gingrich's response to the crime. Oddly, the murdered woman was a single mother on welfare carrying an interracial child, but the murderers were not on welfare, and they were identified as having been reared in "broken homes." "Gingrich is Urged to Butt Out," *San Francisco Chronicle* (Nov. 12, 1995):A10.
2. Rona Berg, quoted in "The Sweet Smell of the '90s," *San Francisco Chronicle* (Aug 16, 1993).
3. The ad appears on the inside cover page of *Gun World* (December 1994).
4. DeParle, "Sheila Burke and the Attack Machine," 35.
5. Andrews, "Panel Votes to Ban Online 'Indecency,' " A3.
6. Gillespie and Schellas, eds, "*Contract With America*," pp. 7–10.
7. Williams, "Different Drummer Please, Marchers!"
8. Shorter, "Yearning for the Family of Yore," 14.
9. Shorter, "Yearning for the Family of Yore," 17.
10. Gordon, *Heroes of their Own Lives*, 3.
11. Gerson, *Hard Choices*, 237.
12. Bureau of Labor Statistics, "Labor Force Participation Unchanged Among Mothers with Young Children."
13. The famous opening line from Tolstoy's *Anna Karenina* is: "All happy families are alike, but each unhappy family is unhappy in its own way."

14. See chapter 8 of Shorter, *The Making of the Modern Family*, which is titled, "Toward the Postmodern Family (or, Setting the Course for the Heart of the Sun)."
15. Dilnot, "What is the Post-Modern?" 245, 249.
16. Stacey, *Brave New Families: Stories of Domestic Upheaval in Late Twentieth Century America.*
17. Popenoe, "Scholars Should Worry About the Disintegration of the American Family," A48; Wilson, "The Family-Values Debate," 24; Lasch, "Misreading the Facts about Families," 136.
18. Seligman, "Variations on a Theme," 38.
19. Belkin, "Bars to Equality of Sexes Seen as Eroding, Slowly," A1, A16. The *Time/CNN* survey data found even greater support for the women's movement: 77% said the movement made life better; only 8% claimed it had made things worse; and 82% said it was still improving the lives of American women. Wallis, "Onward, Women!" 82. Similarly, Furstenberg reports a variety of surveys indicating steady increases in preferences for more egalitarian marriages. "Good Dads, Bad Dads," 207–20.
20. Dance, "Is There a Father in the House?" 25; Shogren, "Republicans Get Lesson in Family Values," C10.
21. Wolfe, *Whose Keeper?* 211.
22. Alexander, *In Praise of Single Parents.*
23. Popenoe, *Disturbing the Nest*, 316–18. Ironically, Popenoe, one of the most active participants in the "neo-family values" campaign that I discuss in chapters 3 and 4, ignores these data in his lament about family decline.
24. Williams, "Different Drummer, Please."

Chapter 1: Backward toward the Postmodern Family

1. The frequency and irregularity of mortality in the premodern period and the economic interdependence of women and men fostered high remarriage rates and the complex kinship relationships these generate. There were also significant regional differences in premodern family patterns. For excellent overviews of the diversity of premodern family patterns, see Stephanie Coontz, *The Social Origins of Private Life*, and Steven Mintz and Susan Kellogg, *Domestic Revolutions.*
2. Alice Kessler-Harris and Karen Sacks consider it doubtful that a majority of working-class men ever earned a family wage. "The Demise of Domesticity."

3. Janet Flammang, "Female Officials in the Feminist Capital." Flammang, "Women Made a Difference," eds. Ira Katznelson and Carole Mueller. Linda Blum, *Between Women and Labor*. Ironically, the San Jose comparable worth strike was called when the feminist mayor and the city council on which women held the majority of seats failed to meet the city employees' demand to proceed on a proposed job study prerequisite to evaluating pay equity.

4. For data on divorce rates and household composition for Santa Clara County in comparison with California and the United States as a whole, see U.S. Bureau of the Census, *Census of Population* for 1960, 1970 and 1980. During the 1970s the county recorded 660 abortions for every 1,000 live births, compared with a statewide average of 489.5 and a ratio of less than 400 for the nation. See U.S. Bureau of the Census, *Statistical Abstract of the United States*.

5. Jean Holland, *The Silicon Syndrome*.

6. Michael S. Malone, "Family in Crisis," 15.

7. For literature describing working-class families as favoring "traditional" gender arrangements, see Mirra Komarovsky, with Jane H. Philips, *Blue-Collar Marriage*; Lillian Rubin, *Worlds of Pain*; Susan Householder Van Horn, *Women, Work and Fertility, 1900–1986*; Theodore Caplow et. al. *Middletown Families*; and Robert Coles and Jane Hallowell Coles, *Women of Crisis*. Barbara Ehrenreich argues that the media constructed this stereotype of the blue-collar working class after it briefly "discovered" this class in 1969. See *Fear of Falling*. I return to this issue below.

8. I employ pseudonyms and change identifying details when describing participants in my study.

9. Judith Stacey and Susan Elizabeth Gerard, "We are not Doormats."

10. There is a great deal of empirical and theoretical support for this view, from feminist psychoanalytic analyses of mothering to time-budget studies of the domestic division of labor. For a direct discussion of women and "the work of kinship," see Micaela di Leonardo, *The Varieties of Ethnic Experience*, pp. 194–205. For an in-depth treatment of domestic labor, see Arlie Hochschild, with Anne Machung, *The Second Shift*.

11. For fuller discussions of this masculinity crisis, see Segal, *Slow Motion*; Griswold, *Fatherhood in America*; Connell, *Masculinities*.

12. Lynne Segal arrives at a similar conclusion. See *Slow Motion*, chapter 2. Patricia Zavella's research on the division of household labor among "Hispano" couples provides additional support for this view. See her

"Sunbelt Hispanics on the Line." A more comprehensive treatment of these issues among Anglo and Hispanic households appears in Louise Lamphere, Felipe Gonzales, Patricia Zavella and Peter Evans, *Working Mothers and Sunbelt Industrialization.*

13. Segal's summary of research on changes in the domestic division of labor supports this view. See *Slow Motion*, chapter 2. And while Arlie Hochschild's recent study of domestic labor emphasizes men's resistance to assuming a fair share of the burden, it also demonstrates that this has become a widely contested issue. See *The Second Shift.*

14. Colleen Leahy Johnson, *Ex-Familia.*

15. On extended, cooperative kin ties among the poor, see Michael Young and Peter Willmott, *Family and Kinship in East London.* David M. Schneider and Raymond T. Smith, *Class Differences and Sex Roles in American Kinship and Family Structure.* Carole Stack, *All Our Kin;* David Halle, *America's Working Man,* 279, takes as a premise the existence of extensive kin ties among blue-collar workers.

16. Stack, *All Our Kin;* Young and Willmott, *Family and Kinship.*

17. Allan Schnaiberg and Sheldon Goldenberg, "From Empty Nest to Crowded Nest," 251–69.

18. On premodern family patterns, see Coontz, *Social Origins of Private Life,* and Mintz and Kellogg, *Domestic Revolutions.*

19. Martha May, "Bread Before Roses: American Workingmen, Labor Unions and The Family Wage." May argues that the demand for a family wage was primarily a class-based demand made by labor unions on behalf of working-class men and their wives in the 19th century, but it was achieved in the 20th century through a cross-class gender alliance between capitalists and unionized men. This analysis helps to resolve a theoretical and political debate among feminist and socialist labor historians concerning the class and gender character of the family wage struggle. Heidi Hartmann, "Capitalism, Patriarchy, and Job Segregation by Sex," criticized the sexist character of the struggle while Jane Humphries, "The Working-Class Family, Women's Liberation and Class Struggle," 25–41, defended the struggle as a form of class and family resistance.

20. After a sharp postwar spurt, divorce rates stabilized only temporarily during the 50s, and above prewar levels. Sar A. Levitan et. al., *What's Happening to American Families?"*, 27. The proportion of women entering college climbed slowly throughout the 1950s, before escalating sharply since the mid-60s: in 1950, 12% of women ages 24–29 had

completed one year of college; this figure rose to 22% in 1965 and reached 43% by 1984. Steven D. McLaughlin et al., *The Changing Lives of American Women*, pp. 33–34. Van Horn, *Women, Work and Fertility*, 194 makes the interesting, provocative argument that a disjuncture between the limited kinds of jobs available to women and the increasing numbers of eduated women seeking jobs during the 1960s helped to regenerate feminism. For additional discussions of the rise of working wives, see Kingsley Davis, "Wives and Work: A Theory of the Sex-Role Revolution and its Consequences," in *Feminism, Children, and the New Families*; Kathleen Gerson, *Hard Choices*; Carl Degler, *At Odds*; Elaine Tyler May, *Homeward Bound*; and Sara Evans, *Born for Liberty*.

21. See Evans, *Born for Liberty*, 253–54; Van Horn, *Women, Work, and Fertility*; Kessler-Harris and Sacks, "Demise of Domesticity."

22. Larry Bumpass and James Sweet, "Preliminary Evidence on Cohabitation," report higher cohabitation rates among those with high school education than among those with college education, and higher divorce rates among those who cohabit prior to marriage. For differential divorce rates by income and race, see also, Van Horn, *Women, Work and Fertility*; Levitan et. al., *What's Happening to the American Family?*; and Henry A. Walker, "Black-White Differences in Marriage and Family Patterns," in Dornbusch and Strober, *Feminism, Children, and the New Families*. A classic ethnography of matrilineal support systems among working-class people is Young and Wilmott, *Family and Kinship in East London*. See also, Schneider and Smith, *Class Differences and Sex Roles*. Stack, *All Our Kin*, is the classic ethnographic portrayal of matrifocal cooperative kin networks among poor African-Americans. However, Linda Gordon, *Heroes of Their Own Lives*, cautions against the tendency to exaggerate and romanticize the existence of extended kinship support systems among the very poor.

23. For data and discussions of non-economic motives for paid employment among blue-collar women, see Mary Lindenstein Walshok, "Occupational Values and Family Roles," in *Working Women and Families*; Gerson, *Hard Choices*; and Kessler-Harris and Sacks, "Demise of Domesticity." Even Komarovsky's early, classic study *Blue-Collar Marriage* discusses the growth of noneconomic motives for employment among the wives of blue-collar men.

24. See Jessie Bernard, *The Future of Marriage*, p. 53 for her famous pronouncement that being a housewife makes many women sick.

25. For example, Barbara Ehrenreich suggests that "the working class, from

the moment of its discovery," by the professional middle class in 1969, "was conceived in masculine terms." (*Fear of Falling*, p. 108.) See also Joan Acker, "Women and Social Stratification."

26. This was one of the understated findings of a study which attempted to operationalize Marxist categories of class. See Eric Olin Wright, Cynthia Costello, David Hacker and Joey Sprague, "The American Class Structure," 709–26.

27. Ehrenreich, *Fear of Falling*, p. 101.

28. Ibid, p. 115.

29. Ibid, p. 223. In December 1989 *Time* magazine ran a cover story on the future of feminism which drew quick, angry rebuttals from many feminists, a response I find out of proportion to the substance or the data in the story. A survey of 1,000 women conducted in 1989 by Yankelovich Clancy Shulman for *Time/CNN* found a smaller proportion of the women sampled, 33%, choosing to identify themselves as "feminists." However, 77% of the women surveyed claimed that the women's movement has made life better, 94% said the movement helped women become more independent, and 82% said it was still improving the lives of American women. Addressing a perceived discrepancy between these data, Claudia Wallis, the story's author opined that "in many ways, feminism is a victim of its own resounding achievements," p. 82. See "Onward, Women!" 80–89.

30. For example, Daniel Bell, *The End of Ideology*, and Seymour Martin Lipset, *Political Man*.

31. Employing conservative measurement techniques designed to understate the extent of income loss, a study of changes in family income found that 40% of American families lost income between 1979 and 1986 and another 20% maintained stable incomes only because employment of wives compensated for falling wages of husbands. Stephen Rose and David Fasenfest, "Family Incomes in the 1970s." See also Newman, *Falling From Grace*; Bennett Harrison and Barry Bluestone, *The Great U-Turn*; Sara Kuhn and Barry Bluestone, "Economic Restructuring and Female Labor"; Joan Smith, "Marginalized Labor Forces During the Reagan Recovery"; Ehrenreich, *Fear of Falling*; Alan Wolfe, *Whose Keeper?* Moreover, measures of income inequality grossly understate the extent of economic inequality in this society. A late 1980s study of the distribution of wealth commissioned by the Census Bureau surveyed assets as well as income and found much graver disparities. For example, the median net worth of the top 1% of American households was 22

times greater than the median net worth of the remaining 99%. David R. Francis, "Study Finds Steep Inequality in Wealth."

32. William Wilson, *The Truly Disadvantaged*, and J. Smith, "Marginalized Labor Forces." One consequence of this is an increasing divergence in the family patterns of whites and African-Americans as marriage rates, in particular, plummet among the latter. See Cherlin, "Marriage, Divorce, Remarriage, 1950s–1980s," 17–18. Francis reports that the median net worth of whites is 11.7 times that of African-Americans. "Study Finds Steep Inequality in Wealth."

33. For a detailed ethnographic treatment of this decline in intergenerational prospects, see Newman, *Declining Fortunes*.

34. Vlae Kershner, "The Payoff for Educated Workers," A2.

35. J. Smith, "Marginalized Labor Forces," 1. See also *The Forgotten Half.*

36. J Smith, "Marginalized Labor Forces," 1; Levitan et. al., *What's Happening to the Family?*, p. 117. Rose and Fasenfast report a 17% decline in absolute earnings between 1979 and 1986 for men with high school educational levels or less. Kershner reports that workers with five or more years of college gained 11% income between 1980 and 1987 while workers with high school diplomas broke even, and those with less education lost at least 5% of their earnings. See also, *The Forgotten Half*; Harrison and Bluestone, *Great U-Turn*. As the size of the standing army has decreased, military recruiters can be much more selective. For example, the U.S. Army Corps now takes very few recruits who do not have a high school diploma.

37. Ehrenreich, *Fear of Falling*, 205.

38. Quoted in Wolfe, *Whose Keeper?*, 65.

39. Eric Olin Wright and Bill Martin, "The Transformation of the American Class Structure, 1960–1980," 1–29; Kuhn and Bluestone, "Economic Restructuring and Female Labor;" Kershner, "Payoff for Educated Workers."

40. Ehrenreich, *Fear of Falling*, 202; Rose and Fasenfest, "Family Incomes in the 1980s," 8. The gap between single and married couple households is even more dramatic when assets are surveyed. A Census Bureau study found the net financial assets of married couple households to be nine times greater than those headed by nonmarried people. (Francis, "Study Finds Steep Inequality in Wealth.")

41. Ehrenreich, *Fear of Falling*, 206. For supportive data, see Wright and Martin, "Transformation of Class Structure."

42. J. Smith, "Marginalized Labor"; Kuhn and Bluestone, "Economic Restructuring and Female Labor"; Kessler-Harris and Sacks, "Demise of Domesticity."

43. See, for example, Frank Furstenberg, "Good Dads, Bad Dads," and Kathleen Gerson, *No Man's Land.*

44. The controversial *Time* cover story on the future of feminism, for example, reports a 1989 survey by Robert Half International in which 56% of men polled said they would forfeit one-fourth of their salaries "to have more family or personal time," and 45% "said they would probably refuse a promotion that involved sacrificing hours with their family." See Zavella, "Sun Belt Hispanics on the Line," for a discussion of the active participation in child care and housework by Hispanic husbands of women who are "mainstay providers" for their households. See Segal, *Slow Motion,* chapters 2 and 10, Gerson, *No Man's Land;* and Griswold, *Fatherhood in America* for fuller discussions of men's changing family lives.

45. "Marriage, Divorce, Remarriage," 17.

46. Between 1960 and 1980 a 43% decline among men between the ages of 20 and 49. Research by Eggebeen and Uhlenberg reported in Furstenberg, "Good Dads, Bad Dads," 201. Furstenberg offers an intelligent, historically-situated analysis of the contradictory evidence on contemporary fatherhood.

47. The 90% datum is reported in Andrew Cherlin's introductory essay to his edited collection, *The Changing American Family and Public Policy,* 8. See Nancy D. Polikoff, "Gender and Child-Custody Determinations" for a careful refutation of the widespread view that women retain an unfair advantage over men in child-custody decisions by divorce courts.

48. Emily Abel, "Adult Daughters and Care for the Elderly," 479–97.

49. Blankenhorn, *Fatherless America,* 101.

50. *Ibid.,* 105.

51. For example, this was the principal concern reported by those surveyed in the study discussed above, p. 8. "Most Regard Family Highly," *New York Times* (October 10, 1989), A18.

52. According to Joan Smith, low-income African-Americans provide the sole exception to this generalization because the majority contain only one possible wage-earner. "Marginalized Labor Forces," p. 1. For Additional data, see, Myra Strober, "Two-Earner Families," in Dornbusch and Strober, eds., *Feminism, Children, and the New Families.*

53. According to Myra Strober, in 1985 42% of households were of this type. "Two-Earner Families," 161. However, Census Bureau data for 1988 report that only 27% of all households included two parents living with children. Quoted in Philip S. Gutis, "What Makes a Family?" B1.
54. Larry Bumpass and Teresa Castro, "Trends in Marital Disruption," 28.

Chapter 2: The Family Is Dead, Long Live Our Families!

1. John Gillis, "Families of Strangers."
2. *The Compact Edition of the Oxford English Dictionary.*
3. Gillis, 7.
4. O.E.D.
5. Gillis, 6.
6. See, for example, Jacqueline Jones, *Labor of Love, Labor of Sorrow.* Paula Giddings, *When and Where I Enter* and Deborah Gray White, *Ar'n't I a Woman?*
7. Deniz Kandiyoti, "Bargaining With Patriarchy," 274–90.
8. See, Barbara Welter, "The Cult of True Womanhood, 1820–1860," Mary Ryan, *The Empire of the Mother* and Barbara Epstein, *The Politics of Domesticity.*
9. Michael Grossberg, "Who Gets the Child?", 235–60.
10. The classic formulation of this thesis appears in William J. Goode, *World Revolution and Family Patterns.*
11. This perspective is identified with the Cambridge Group for the History of Population and Social Structure. See, for example, Peter Laslett, *The World We Have Lost.*
12. For example, the Mashpee of Cape Cod, Massachusetts suffered this disruption. See, James Clifford, "Identity in Mashpee." See also, Michael Yellowbird and C. Matthew Snipp, "American Indian Families."
13. James Ferguson, "Migration, mineworkers, and 'the modern family.' "
14. Barbara Ehrenreich, *Fear of Falling.*
15. For the initial argument that the struggle for the male breadwinner wage represented collusion between male workers and bosses, and thus between patriarchy and capitalism, see Heidi Hartmann, "Capitalism, Patriarchy and Job Segregation by Sex." Jane Humphries challenged this analysis with the claim that working-class wives supported their husbands' *class* struggle for the family wage, in "The Working-Class Family, Women's Liberation and Class Struggle," 25–41. More recent

work has refined and complicated this analysis. See, for example, Martha May, "Bread Before Roses."

16. For data and fuller analyses of these processes see, Robert Griswold, *Fatherhood in America*, and Judith Stacey, *Brave New Families*.

17. Katja Boh, "European Family Life Patterns—A Reappraisal," 280.

18. Moreover, since 1990 almost twice as many women as men have been added to the paid workforce. "Working Wives Keep America's Families Out of Red," A5.

19. A 1992 study found that the rate of unwed motherhood among women who had attended at least a year of college rose from 5.5% in 1982 to 11.3% in 1992. The rate for women with professional or managerial jobs, like Murphy Brown, rose from 3.1% to 8.3%. However, in 1993, 47% of families headed by single mothers lived in poverty, compared with 8.3% of two-parent families. Jason DeParle, "Census Reports a Sharp Increase Among Never-Married Mothers," A1, 9.

20. *The World's Women 1970–1990*.

21. Two of the most alarmist interpretations of family decline in Sweden are, David Popenoe, *Disturbing the Nest: Family Change and Decline in Modern Society* and Allan Carlson, *The Swedish Experiment in Family Politics*.

22. Stephen Kinzer, "$650 a Baby," A1.

23. In 1988, appx 22% of children lived in single parent families, 47% lived in dual worker families, and 29% lived in male breadwinner, female homemaker families. Griswold, op. cit., 220. However, by 1993, 30% of births in the United States were to unwed mothers. Kristin A. Moore, "Report to Congress on Out-Of-Wedlock Childbearing."

24. Timothy M. Smeeding, "Why the U.S. Antipoverty System Doesn't Work Very Well."

25. Same-sex partners who choose to legalize their relationship are entitled to most of the rights and benefits of heterosexual marriage. However, they are not entitled to a church marriage or to adopt children.

26. For comparative data, see, Smeeding, op. cit; and Irene Wennemo, *Sharing the Costs of Children*.

27. Gordon, *Pitied But Not Entitled*.

28. Smeedling, op. cit.

29. See Daniel Patrick Moynihan, "Congress Builds a Coffin," 33–36.

30. See Susan Reinhold, "Through The Parliamentary Looking Glass," 61–78.

31. Perhaps the best-known essay of the centrist family-values campaign is

Barbara Defoe Whitehead, "Dan Quayle Was Right." I discuss this campaign in chapters 3 and 4.

32. Harold Wilensky, "Common Problems, Divergent Policies," 1–3.
33. Quotes were taken from the "Guiding Principles On The Family," and "Family in Crisis."
34. Judith Stacey, *Patriarchy and Socialist Revolution in China.*
35. New York, Museum of Modern Art.

Chapter 3: The Neo-Family Values Campaign

1. Whitehead, "Dan Quayle Was Right," 47–84.
2. Whitehead, "Was Dan Quayle Right?" 13. For sample retreads, see, Charen, "Hey, Murphy, Quayle was right," and Fields, "Murphy's chorus of enlightened celebrities," p. B9.
3. Popenoe, "The Controversial Truth: Two-Parent Families Are Better;" Popenoe, "Scholars Should Worry about the Disintegration of the American Family;" Beck, "What's good for babies: Both parents."
4. Moynihan, "Defining Deviancy Down," 17–30; Wilson, "The Family-Values Debate," 24–31.
5. Stacey, *Brave New Families.*
6. Fields, "Murphy's Chorus," B9.
7. Popenoe, "Scholars Should Worry," A48. For the statement and list of Council members, see "Family and Child Well-Being: Eight Propositions," 11.
8. Personal interview conducted April 6, 1994, Oakland, California.
9. Quoted in Karen Winkler, "Communitarians Move Their Ideas Outside Academic Arena," A7.
10. Kamarck and Galston, "Putting Children First."
11. Blankenhorn, Elshtain, and Bayme, eds., *Rebuilding the Nest*; National Commission on Children, *Beyond Rhetoric.*
12. Personal interview, April 6, 1994.
13. Whitehead, "A New Familism?" 5.
14. Wilson, "The Family-Values Debate," 31.
15. Klein, "The Out-of-Wedlock Question," 37.
16. Blankenhorn made these remarks during his presentation to "Safe Communities: A Search For Solutions," a 1995 California Public Affairs Forum sponsored by Hitachi, Ltd., which was held at the Sheraton Palace Hotel, San Francisco, September 28, 1995.
17. Quoted in Michael Kranish, "In bully pulpit, preaching values," 17.

18. Wilson, "The Family-Values Debate," 24.
19. The debate took place on an ABC radio call-in program, "The Gil Gross Show," broadcast on Jan 18, 1993.
20. Whitehead, "Dan Quayle Was Right," 47.
21. Ibid, 80.
22. Wilson, "The Family-Values Debate," 31. Syndicated columnist Suzanne Field abridged Whitehead's *Atlantic* story, charging that Dan Quayle was punished like a messenger in a Greek tragedy when he attacked Murphy Brown, "knocked about for delivering bad news that contradicted the biases of the media, the morality chic of the beautiful people, and the scholarship of ideological feminists, among others." After ridiculing media stars who spoke up for Murphy Brown, Field remarked, "We can't expect wisdom from celebrities, but feminist academics at good universities peddle similar claptrap. Sociologist Judith Stacey of UC, Davis describes a postmodern future for women in which none of us are oppressed by the nuclear family. Field, "Murphy's Chorus," 89.
23. Gillis suggested the term during a discussion of an early draft of this paper with the "family values" seminar at the Center for Advanced Studies in the Social and Behavioral Sciences, November 29, 1993.
24. Popenoe, "The Controversial Truth."
25. Whitehead, "Dan Quayle Was Right," 48.
26. Whitehead, "The Expert's Story of Marriage," quoted in Moynihan, "Defining Deviancy Down," 24.
27. *Beyond Rhetoric* cites essays by Blankenhorn, Elshtain, Popenoe, Sylvia Hewlett, and other contributors to Blankenhorn, Elshtain and Bayme, eds., *Rebuilding the Nest.*
28. Popenoe, "Scholars should worry."
29. Council on Families in America, "Family and Child Well-Being: Eight Propositions," p. 11.
30. Popenoe, "Controversial Truth."
31. To sample the diversity of scholarly views, see a careful evaluation of the inconclusive findings of research on the impact of divorce on children, Furstenberg, and Cherlin, *Divided Families.* For a review of the research on gay and lesbian parenting, see Patterson, "Children of Lesbian and Gay Parents," 1025–42. Indeed, even Sara McLanahan, who Whitehead's *Atlantic* essay portrayed as recanting her earlier views on the benign effects of single parenting, provides a more nuanced analysis of the sources of whatever disadvantages the children of single parents

experience than Whitehead leads readers to believe. She acknowledges that research does not demonstrate that children of "mother only" households would have been better off if their two biological parents had married or never divorced. See McLanahan and Booth, "Mother-Only Families: Problems, Prospects, and Politics," 557–80.

32. Demo, "Parent-Child Relations: Assessing Recent Changes," 104.
33. Ibid., 110.
34. Wallerstein and Kelly, *Surviving the Breakup*; Wallerstein and Blakeslee, *Second Chances.*
35. Demo, "Parent-Child Relations," 110. For an even more comprehensive, balanced survey of research on the impact of divorce on children see Furstenberg and Cherlin, *Divided Families.*
36. See Furstenberg and Cherlin for a summary of this research.
37. Murray, "The Time has Come to put a Stigma Back on Illegitimacy."
38. Murray appeared on "This Week With David Brinkley," November 29, 1993. The op-ed by Hoover Institute scholar, John Bunzel, aired on, "Perspective," KQED-FM, San Francisco, December 21, 1993.
39. Blankenhorn, *Rebuilding the Nest*, 21.
40. Quoting from an essay he wrote in 1965, Moynihan, "Defining Deviancy Down," 26.
41. Wilson, "The Family-Values Debate," 31.
42. Klein, "The Out-of Wedlock Question," 37.
43. The quotes from Shalala and the unidentified liberal appear in Klein, "Out-of-Wedlock Question."
44. See, Kamarck and Galston, "Putting Children First: A Progressive Family Policy for the 1990s," 9.
45. Many feminists fear that even employing the concept "postfeminism" cedes important political ground to the backlash. I disagree and use the term to indicate a culture that has both assimilated and tamed many of the basic ideas of second-wave feminism. For a fuller discussion of this use of this term, see Rosenfelt and Stacey, "Second Thoughts on the Second Wave."
46. Popenoe, "Scholars Should Worry."
47. Blankenhorn, *Rebuilding the Nest*, 19.
48. Wilson, 31.
49. Whitehead, "A Few Familism?" 2.
50. Shellbanger, "Bill Galston Tells the President," B1.
51. Lefkowitz, "Where Dad Belongs," A12.
52. Chira, "Push to Revamp Ideal for American Fathers," 10. Blankenhorn

presents an extended, polemical exposition of his neotraditional father-hood ideology in his *Fatherless America*. Blankenhorn's ideology has become too conservative even for some of his colleagues at the Institute for American Values. Originally Popenoe and Blankenhorn contracted to co-author *Fatherless America*, but due to ideological differences, Popenoe wrote his own book on this subject, *Life Without Father*, which has just been released in April 1996, as this book is going to press.

53. For my earlier critiques of Elshtain, Friedan and Hewlett, see, Stacey, "The New Conservative Feminism;" and Rosenfelt and Stacey, "Second Thoughts on the Second Wave."

54. Blankenhorn, for example, is interpreted approvingly by a *Wall Street Journal* columnist as providing intellectual justification for, "laws that mandate spousal notification prior to all abortions. Today laws in most states consider fetuses the property of pregnant women. Unfortunately, this posture leads to the view that children are the sole responsibility of mothers." Lefkowitz, "Where Dad Belongs."

55. Quoted in Winkler, "Communitarians Move Their Ideas Outside Academic Arena," A13.

56. Whitehead, "A New Familism?" 2.

57. Popenoe, "Modern Marriage: Revising the Cultural Script," 2.

58. Blankenhorn, *Fatherless America*, 122.

59. Glenn, "A Plea for Objective Assessment of the Notion of Family Decline," 543; Wilson, "Family-Values Debate," 25.

60. Clinton, *It Takes A Village*, p. 43.

61. Johnson, "No-Fault Divorce Is Under Attack," A8.

62. Ibid.

63. Weitzman, *The Divorce Revolution* is the most significant treatment of no-fault divorce.

64. Ahrons, *The Good Divorce*, p. 35.

65. Popenoe applies this term to me and other critics of "family-values" ideology in, "Scholars Should Worry."

66. Glenn, "Plea for an Objective View," 544.

67. Wilson, "Family-Values Debate," 29.

68. Popenoe, "American Family Decline, 1960–1990," 529.

69. Moynihan, "Defining Deviancy Down," 26; Whitehead, "Dan Quayle Was Right," 70.

70. Blankenhorn, *Fatherless America*, 233.

71. Elshtain, "Family and Civic Life," 130.

72. See pp. 128–38.

73. Moynihan quoted in Winkler, "Communitarians Move Their Ideas," A13.
74. Batteiger, "Bigotry for Bucks," 19. For primary evidence of the prominence of homophobic appeals in rightwing organizing, see, for example, James C. Dobson, "1993 in Review," Focus on the Family Newsletter, January 1994.
75. White, "Christian Right Tries to Capitalize on Anti-Gay Views." A6.
76. Toner, "Republican Factions Gather Under One Tent, Then Argue."
77. See above, p. 55.
78. Traube, "Family Matters, 63."
79. Moynihan, *The Negro Family*.
80. Murray, "The emerging white underclass and how to save it," A15.
81. Odum, *Social and Mental Traits of the Negro*, quoted in Gutman, "Persistent Myths about the Afro-American Family," 184.
82. Wilson defines this index as the ratio of employed Black males per 100 Black females in the same age group. He charts a decline in this ratio from 70 in 1960 to 40 in 1986, and the disparity is reflected in the decline of Black marriage rates. William J. Wilson, *The Truly Disadvantaged*.
83. Married voters ages 18–34 with children voted 48% for Bush, 39% for Clinton and 22% for Perot; singles (with and without children) in that age group voted 58% for Clinton, 20% for Bush, and 19% for Perot. Poll data were reported in a *Washington Post* story, by Vobejda reprinted as, " 'Family Gap' Found in Post-Election Poll," A4.
84. Bauer, "Family Values Matter!" 16.
85. Suggs and Carter, "Cincinnati's Odd Couple," A11.
86. *San Francisco Chronicle* (December 23, 1993).
87. Smothers, "Tell It to Mom, Dad and the Authorities," 2. For an astute analysis of media treatment of the Newark car theft panic, see Gregory, "Time To Make The Doughnuts: On the Politics of Subjugation in the 'Inner City,' " (Paper presented at American Anthropological Association Meetings, Washington, D.C., November 1993).
88. Whitehead, "Dan Quayle Was Right," 55.
89. Academic feminists indulge this impulse as well. For a recent example, see Probyn's otherwise incisive critique of postfeminist TV family fare, "Television's *Unheimlich* Home."
90. Derber, "Coming Glued: Communitarianism to the Rescue," 27–30.
91. For example, in a 1985 Roper poll, 51% of women claimed that given the choice, they would prefer a paid job to fulltime homemaking, but in

1991 only 43% of women expressed that preference, while 53% said they would rather stay home. Nancy Gibbs, "The War Against Feminism," p. 55.

92. Hochschild, "Inside the Clockwork of Male Careers," 47–81.

93. See discussion above, p. 13.

94. Popenoe, "The Family Condition of America: Cultural Change and Public Policy," 98. See also, Wilson, "The Family-Values Debate," 30: "Marriage is in large measure a device for reining in the predatory sexuality of males." While, according to Gilder, "Men without women frequently become the 'single menace,' . . . "often destined to a Hobbsean life—solitary, poor, nasty, brutish, and short." Gilder, *Men and Marriage* 6–7, 10. For a feminist reading of the social evolutionary domestication of men, see Ortner, "The Virgin and the State," 19–35.

95. Presentation to the Berkeley Family Research and Public Policy Seminar, March 1995. The draft legislation is available from Prof. Bruch, King Law School, University of California, Davis.

96. Ehrenreich, "Two, Three, Many Husbands," 183–87.

97. Schwartz, "Children's New Bonds: Para-Dads, Para-Moms," B1, B4.

98. For an astute and moving account of the experiences of some of the heroic doctors who have paid these costs, see Joffe, *Doctors of Conscience.*

Chapter 4: Virtual Social Science and the Politics of Family Values

1. Moynihan, *The Negro Family.*

2. Gillis, "What's Behind the Debate on Family Values?".

3. However, recently politicians in Britain and elsewhere in Europe have initiated efforts to stir public concern over single motherhood, divorce and family instability. See Tuula Gordon, "Single Women and Familism," and Jane Millar, "State, Family and Personal Responsibility: The Changing Balance for Lone Mothers in the United Kingdom." For example, the headline story run by London's *Daily Express* on June 23, 1994, Paul Crosbie, "The Crumbling of Family life," seems a direct replica of U.S. rhetoric.

4. In 1994 the Sex and Gender section had 1271 members, which was more than 200 members greater than the section on Medical Sociology, which is currently the second largest specialty section of the A.S.A. (Data provided by American Sociological Association.)

5. Cheal, *Family and the State of Theory,* 8.
6. Parsons and Bales, *Family, Socialization and Interaction Process.*
7. Goode, *World Revolution and Family Patterns.*
8. Friedan, *The Feminine Mystique.*
9. Bernard, *The Future of Marriage.*
10. Mainardi, "The Politics of Housework"; Koedt, "The Myth of the Vaginal Orgasm"; Oakley, *The Sociology of Housework,* and Rubin, "The Traffic in Women: Notes on the Political Economy of Sex."
11. After all, Moynihan's analysis of Black family decline had built quite directly on the sociological work of E. Franklin Frazier, and even *Tally's Corner,* Elliot Liebow's decidedly liberal and sympathetic ethnography of urban Black families, supported the thesis of Black family pathology.
12. Glenn, "The Re-evaluation of Family Change by American Social Scientists," 2.
13. Ibid., 3.
14. Ibid., 4–5.
15. Cherlin, *Marriage, Divorce, Remarriage,* 138.
16. Wallerstein and Blakeslee, *Second Chances: Men, Women, and Children a Decade After Divorce.*
17. McLanahan, *The Consequences of Single Motherhood*; and McLanahan and Bumpass, "Intergenerational Consequences of Family Disruption."
18. Glenn, 10.
19. Marcus, "Power/Knowledge Shifts in America's Present Fin-De-Siècle: A Proposal for a School of American Research Advanced Seminar." The papers produced for the seminar, which was held at the S.A.R. in Santa Fe, NM in November 1994, will appear in Marcus, ed., *New Locations.*
20. For example, as a speaker on an evening plenary session attended by more than one thousand sociologists at the American Sociological Association meetings in Los Angeles in August 1994, Patricia Hill Collins delivered a polemical assault on postmodern theory and was rewarded with rapturous applause.
21. Popenoe, "What's Behind the Family Values Debate?"
22. Ibid.
23. While the proportion of doctoral degrees awarded to women in all fields in the U.S. rose only from 30% in 1980 to 36% in 1990 (National Research Council 1991), in sociology, women's share of Ph.D. degrees rose much more substantially, from 33% in 1977 to 51% in 1989 (National Science Foundation 1991). The American Sociological Association reports that by 1991, 57% of students enrolled in doctoral programs

in sociology in the U.S. were women as were 53% of the members of the A.S.A. The association does not report data on the proportion of women and men in each of the specialty sections, but all who have attended sessions and meetings of the Sex and Gender section and the Family section can confirm the contrast in the relative paucity of men in the former. Sociologist Barrie Thorne, a past president of the Sex and Gender section and a past vice-president of the A.S.A. reports that men have never comprised even 10% of the membership in the former. (personal communication).

24. Weber, *The Sociology of Charismatic Authority*.
25. See Rosenfelt and Stacey, "Second Thoughts on the Second Wave."
26. Glenn, "The Reevaluation of Family Change," 12.
27. Friedan's *The Second Stage* celebrated the reappearance of familism among feminists. For an early critical discussion of the emergence of this perspective within feminism, see Stacey, "The New Conservative Feminism," and "Are Feminists Afraid to Leave Home?"
28. Glenn, "Reevaluation of Family Change," 12.
29. See Sanqvist and Andersson, "Thriving Families in the Swedish Welfare State."
30. For example, he co-convened an academic conference on family change at Stanford University and then coedited the resulting conference volume (Blankenhorn, Elshtain and Bayme 1990). Blankenhorn also spoke at a Santa Clara University conference, "Ethics, Public Policy and the Future of the Family," on April 18, 1995.
31. Hewlett, *A Lesser Life*.
32. Quoted in Winkler, "Communitarians Move Their Ideas Outside Academic Arena."
33. However, Elshtain herself rarely forfeits an opportunity to raise the ante of animus. In a letter to the editor which *The Nation* published in abridged form, Elshtain "hooted" her response to my critical discussion of the centrist campaign, "The New Family-Values Crusaders," that had appeared in the magazine in quite personalized, and purple, prose: "I was pleased to see that Judith Stacey is on the job. Not having been attacked by Ms. Stacey in print for a few years, I wondered if she was still up to the ideological stalking so characteristic of her efforts a few years back. Then, if memory serves, Stacey expended a good bit of energy before finally landing on the label, "New Conservative Feminist" for a few of us and now, to my surprise, I get to be something brand new and exciting, a "New Family Values Crusader." Stacey seems to believe

nothing can be discussed unless you first line people up in team jerseys. This labeling fetishism, alas, has long been characteristic of segments of the sectarian left and this same infantilizing urgency has infected a good bit of academic feminism."

34. For example Cherlin; Furstenburg and Cherlin, *Divided Families*; and even McLanahan.

35. Carlson, *The Swedish Experiment in Family Politics*, 194.

36. Glenn, for example, depicts himself as "among the relatively small number of American family social scientists who believe that some of the changes can be halted if not reversed. Reconstitution of the American family of the 1950s—a goal of some conservatives—is indeed unrealistic and, in my view, undesirable." "Revaluation of Family Change," 11–12.

37. *Here To Stay* is the title of Mary Jo Bane's early, misleadingly optimistic assessment of nuclear family stability in the U.S. that is a frequent foil for the family values campaign.

38. Messer-Davidow, "Manufacturing the Attack on Liberalized Higher Education."

39. Berke, "U.S. Voters Focus on Selves, Poll Says."

40. Yoachum, "Small Minority Voter Turnout A product of Apathy and Anger." In California, whites constituted only 57% of the adult population in the state, but they cast 83% of the votes in the 1994 election.

41. Brownstein, "Democrats Find the Right's Stuff: Family Values."

42. Berke, "Two Top Republicans Soften Their Tone."

43. Ibid.

44. Ibid.

45. Sennett, "The New Censorship," 490.

46. Indeed, survey data indicate an alarming anomaly. On the one hand, since the 1980s "the electorate as a whole moved in a clearly liberal direction on three issues besides gay rights: abortion, the role of women, and, to a lesser extent, on the role of government in guaranteeing jobs and living standards." (Strand and Sherrill, "Electoral Bugaboos? The Impact of Attitudes Toward Gay Rights and Feminism on the 1992 Presidential Vote.") Nonetheless, in a November 1994 poll sponsored by the Democratic Leadership Council, more voters identified the Republicans than the Democrats as the party that "would do a better job strengthening families." Greenberg Research.

47. Fiske, *Media Matters*.

48. Spigel, *Make Room for TV*, and "From the dark ages to the golden age;" also Taylor, *Primetime Families.*
49. See May, *Homeward Bound.*

Chapter 5: Gay and Lesbian Families Are Here

1. With all due credit and apologies to Queer Nation and ACT-UP for adapting their slogan: "We're Here, We're Queer, Get Used to It!"
2. The estimate that at least six million children were living with a gay parent by 1985 appeared in Schulenberg, *Gay Parenting*, and has been accepted or revised upwards by most scholars since then. See, for example, Bozett, 39; Patterson, "Children of Lesbian and Gay Parents;" Allen and Demo, "The Families of Lesbians and Gay Men: A New Frontier in Family Research."
3. Burke, *Family Values: A Lesbian Mother's Fight for Her Son.*
4. Goldenberg, "Virtual Marriages for Same-Sex Couples."
5. Many gay activist groups and scholars, however, have begun to reclaim the term "queer" as a badge of pride, in much the same way that the Black power movement of the 1960s reclaimed the formerly derogatory term for blacks.
6. Reagan and Schlafly both have gay sons, Powell has a lesbian daughter, and Gingrich has a lesbian half-sister.
7. For a sensitive discussion of the definitional difficulties involved in research on gay and lesbian families, see Allen and Demo, "Families of Lesbians and Gay Men," 112–13.
8. See the introduction and chapters one and two of this book for a direct discussion of the postmodern family condition. In Stacey, *Brave New Families*, I provide a booklength, ethnographic treatment of postmodern family life in the Silicon Valley.
9. I explain my use of the term "modern" family above in the Introduction, pp. 6–8, chapter one, pp. 18–19, and chapter two, pp. 38–43.
10. Most gay and lesbian scholars and activists reject the term "homosexual" because it originated within a medical model that classified homosexuality as a sexual perversion or disease and because the term emphasizes sexuality as at the core of the individual's identity. In this chapter, I follow the generally preferred contemporary practice of using the terms "lesbians" and "gay men," but I also occasionally employ the term "gay" generically to include both women and men. I also play with the multiple, and currently shifting, meanings of the term "queer," by

specifying whether I am using the term in its older pejorative sense, in its newer sense of proudly challenging fixed notions of gender and sexuality, or in its more colloquial sense of simply "odd."

11. For historical and cross-cultural treatments of same-sex marriages, relationships, and practices in the West and elsewhere, see, Boswell, *Same-Sex Unions in Premodern Europe*; and Eskridge Jr., "A History of Same-Sex Marriage."

12. Rivera, "Legal Issues in Gay and Lesbian Parenting."

13. Among the influential feminist works of this genre were: Chodorow, *The Reproduction of Mothering*; Gilligan, *In a Different Voice*; and Ruddick, *Maternal Thinking*.

14. See Introduction, p. 5, chapter 3, p. 53, and chapter 4, pp. 83–85.

15. See Rosenbloom, ed., *Unspoken Rules: Sexual Orientation and Women's Human Rights* 226, (fn22); and Benkov, *Reinventing the Family*, 117.

16. Wikler and Wikler, "Turkey-baster Babies," 10.

17. Ibid.

18. In "Junior" a 1994 Christmas season "family film" release, Schwarzenneger plays a research scientist who becomes pregnant as part of experimental fertility research.

19. The first known custody battle involving a lesbian couple and a sperm donor was "Loftin v. Flournoy" in California. For a superb discussion of the relevant case law, see Polikoff, "This Child Does Have Two Mothers."

20. Polikoff, "Two Mothers" provides detailed discussion of the most significant legal cases of custody contests after death of biological lesbian co-mother. In both the most prominent cases, higher courts eventually reversed decisions that had denied custody to the surviving lesbian parent, but only after serious emotional harm had been inflicted on the children and parents alike. See pp. 527–32.

21. Henry, "A Tale of Three Women," 297.

22. Ibid., 300; and Polikoff, "This Child Does Have Two Mothers," 492.

23. Griscom, "The Case of Sharon Kowalski and Karen Thompson."

24. See Rubenstein, *Lesbians, Gay Men, and the Law*, 452.

25. For a fascinating discussion of the political compromises involved in the Danish case, see Miller, *Out in the World*, chap. 12.

26. However, the highest courts in Vermont, Massachusetts and New York now allow unmarried couples, including lesbian and gay male couples, to jointly adopt a child. In November 1995 the highly divided NY top court reached this decision which explicitly acknowledged "fundamen-

tal changes" in US family life and its significance for gay parents. See Dao, "Ruling Lets Unwed Couples Adopt," A11.

27. National Center for Lesbian Rights, "Our Day in Court—Against Each Other," in Rubenstein, 561–2.

28. de Lamadrid, p. 178.

29. In 1994 Sharon Bottoms lost custody of her two-year-old son because the trial court judge deemed her lesbianism to be immoral and illegal. In April 1995 the Virginia state supreme court upheld the ruling, which at this writing is being appealed to the U.S. Supreme Court.

30. Quoted in Sherman, ed. *Lesbian and Gay Marriage*, 191.

31. Ibid., 173.

32. Bozett, epilogue to *Gay and Lesbian Parents*, 232.

33. Cited in Sherman, *Lesbian and Gay Marriage*, 9, fn 6. A more recent poll conducted by *The Advocate* suggests that the trend of support for gay marriage is increasing. See Wolfson, "Crossing the Threshold," 583.

34. Terry announced his plans January 24, 1996 on "Randall Terry Live," and LaHaye made her pitch the next day, January 25, 1996 on "Beverly LaHaye Live."

35. Dunlap, "Some States Trying to Stop Gay Marriages before They Start," A18; Dunlap, "Fearing a Toehold for Gay Marriage, Conservatives Rush to Bar the Door," A7. Lockhead, "GOP Bill Targets Same-Sex Marriages, *San Francisco Chronicle*, My 9, 1996, A1, 15.

36. Ibid, A1.

37. Press Briefing by Mike McCurry, White House, My 14, 1996, Office of the Press Secretary.

38. "Vatican Denounces Gay-Marriage Idea." *New York Times*, Mar 29, 1996, A8.

39. Dunlap, "Reform Rabbis Vote to Back Gay Marriage," A8.

40. "The Freedom to Marry." *New York Times*, April 7, 1996, Editorials/Letters, p. 10.

41. The decision stated that the sexual orientation of the parties was irrelevant, because same-sex spouses could be of any sexual orientation. It was the gender discrimination involved in limiting one's choice of spouse that violated the state constitution. See Wolfson, "Crossing the Threshold," 573.

42. Polikoff, "We Will Get What We Ask For: Why Legalizing Gay and Lesbian Marriage Will Not 'Dismantle the Legal Structure of Gender in Every Marriage'."

43. Law Professor, Thomas Coleman, who is executive director of the

"Family Diversity Project" in California, expresses these views in Sherman, 128–9.

44. Sullivan, "The Conservative Case for Gay Marriage;" Rauch, "A Pro-Gay, Pro-Family Policy."
45. Tede Matthews in Sherman, 57.
46. Kirk Johnson quoted in Wolfson, 567.
47. Hunter, "Marriage, Law and Gender," 12.
48. Wolfson, "Crossing the Threshold."
49. Mohr, *A More Perfect Union*, 48, 41, 50.
50. "Some Progress Found in Poll on Gay Rights," *San Francisco Chronicle*, June 20, 1994.
51. Ryan, "No Easy Way Out," 90. Sullivan, "Here Comes the Groom."
52. Rauch, "Pro-Gay, Pro-Family Policy."
53. Herscher, "After Reconsidering, Montana Junks Gay Sex Bill," A2.
54. See chap. 3, pp. 69–71 above.
55. Clinton, according to his senior adviser George Stephanopoulos, "thinks the proper role for the government is to work on the fight against discrimination, but he does not believe we should support (gay) marriage." Quoted in Sandalow and Tuller, "White House Tells Gays It Backs Them," A2.
56. Clinton, *It Takes A Village*, book jacket copy.
57. Remafedi, *Death by Denial.*
58. Quoted in Miller, *Out in the World*, 350.
59. This is the title and central argument of Popenoe's *New York Times* op-ed discussed above in the Introduction, p. 8 and chapter 3, pp. 53–57.
60. Wolfson, "Crossing the Threshold," 599.
61. The three journals were *Journal of Marriage and the Family, Family Relations*, and *Journal of Family Issues.* Allen & Demo, "Families of Lesbians and Gay Men," 119.
62. For overviews of the research, see Patterson, "Children of Lesbian and Gay Parents;" Laird, "Lesbian and Gay Families;" and Allen and Demo, "Families of Lesbians and Gay Men."
63. Laird, "Lesbian and Gay Families," 316–17.
64. *Ibid.*, 317; Demo and Allen "Diversity within lesbian and gay families," 26; Patterson, "Children of Lesbians and Gay Men;" Tasker and Golombok, "Adults Raised as Children in Lesbian Families."
65. Tasker and Golombok, "Adults Raised as Children in Lesbian Families."

66. Quoted in Rafkin, *Different Mothers*, 34.
67. Laird, "Lesbian and Gay Families."
68. See, for example, Patterson; Demo and Allen; Benkov; Weston; and Peplau.
69. Minton, "U.S.A.," in Rosenbloom, *Unspoken Rules*, p. 219.
70. Quoted in Maralee Schwartz & Kenneth J. Cooper, "Equal Rights Initiative in Iowa Attacked," *Washington Post*, Aug 23, 1992, p. A15.
71. Laird, pp. 315–16.
72. See, for example, Williams, *The Spirit and the Flesh*.
73. As Tasker and Golombok concede, "Young adults from lesbian homes tended to be more willing to have a sexual relationship with someone of the same gender if they felt physically attracted to them. They were also more likely to have considered the possibility of developing same-gender sexual attractions or relationships. Having a lesbian mother, therefore, appeared to widen the adolescent's view of what constituted acceptable sexual behavior to include same-gender sexual relationships." 212.
74. Rich, "Compulsory Heterosexuality and the Lesbian Continuum."
75. Sedgwick, "How to Bring Your Kids Up Gay," in Warner, ed., *Fear of a Queer Planet*, 76.
76. Quoted in Rafkin, *Different Mothers*, 64–5.
77. Shannon Minter, "United States," in Rosenbloom, *Unspoken Rules*, 222.
78. Remafedi, *Death by Denial*.
79. Quoted in Sherman, 70.
80. Due, *Joining The Tribe*.
81. See Irvine, "A Place in the Rainbow: Theorizing Lesbian and Gay Culture," 232.
82. Quoted in Rafkin, *Different Mothers*, 24.
83. Quoted in Polikoff, "This Child Does have Two Mothers," 569–70.
84. Quoted in Polikoff, 570.
85. Quoted in Rafkin, 81.
86. Benkov, *Reinventing the Family*, chap. 8.
87. Kurdek and Schmitt, "Relationship Quality of Gay Men in Closed or Open Relationships"; Lynch, "Nonghetto Gays: An Ethnography of Suburban Homosexuals" in Herdt, ed., *Gay Culture in America*.
88. Rafkin, 39.
89. Allen and Demo.
90. Polikoff, "This Child Does Have Two Mothers," 461 (fn. 2).
91. Weston, "Parenting in the Age of AIDS," 159.

92. Blankenhorn, *Fatherless America*, 233; Leo, "Promoting no-dad families," 26; Seligson, "Seeds of Doubt," 28.
93. Bozett, p. 4 discusses gay male parenthood strategies.
94. Demo & Allen, "Diversity within gay and lesbian families." 26. Also see Laird.
95. Quoted in Rafkin, 33.
96. Ibid., 53.
97. Ibid., 174.
98. See Newton, "A Feminist Among Promise Keepers," A6; Segal, *Slow Motion*; Ehrensaft, *Parenting Together*.
99. Shared parenting between women and men was a favored political goal that many feminists deduced from such 1970s works of feminist theory as Dinnerstein, *The Mermaid and the Minotaur* and Chodorow, *Reproduction of Mothering*. Ehrensaft, *Parenting Together* provides a balanced treatment of some of the paradoxes, difficulties and achievements of shared parenting efforts. Joint custody, however, which many feminists first favored, has often been used to reduce child support and financial settlements.
100. Downey and Powell, "Do Children in Single-Parent Households Fare Better Living With Same-Sex Parents?"
101. Fairbank, Maslin, Maullin & Associates, "National Health and Safety Study," pp. 8, 10.
102. Kurdek, "The Allocation of Household Labor in Gay, Lesbian, and Heterosexual Married Couples;" Blumstein and Schwartz, *American Couples*; Peplau, 193.
103. Peplau, 193; Blumstein and Schwartz.
104. Blumstein and Schwartz, Peplau, Laird.
105. See Weston, *Families We Choose*, for an ethnographic treatment of these chosen kin ties.
106. As Allen and Demo suggest, "an aspect of biculturalism is resilience and creative adaptation in the context of minority group oppression and stigma," and this "offers a potential link to other oppressed groups in American society." "The Families of Lesbians and Gay Men," 122.

EPIGRAPH SOURCES

Introduction

1. Governor Edgar quoted in, "Gingrich is Urged to Butt Out," *San Francisco Chronicle*, November 23, 1995: A10.
2. Governor Wilson quoted in, Doug Willis, "Wilson to unveil welfare and pro-family reforms," *Sacramento Bee*, January 8, 1996: A1–2.
3. Pat Robertson quoted in Maralee Schwartz & Kenneth J. Cooper, "Equal Rights Initiative in Iowa Attacked," *Washington Post*, August 23, 1992: A15.

Chapter 4
Epigraphs on page 83

1. Senator Moynihan quoting his 1965 work in a fundraising letter mailed in October 1994.
2. Quayle quoted in Susan Yoachum, "Quayle Talks Tough on Fatherhood," *San Francisco Chronicle*, September 9, 1994: A1, 17.
3. President Clinton quoted in, "In Baptist Talk Clinton Stresses Moral Themes," *New York Times*, September 10, 1994: A1, 6.

Epigraphs on page 88

1. John Gillis, "What's Behind the Debate on Family Values?" Paper delivered at American Sociological Association Meetings, Los Angeles, August 6, 1994.
2. Norval Glenn, "The Re-evaluation of Family Change by American Social Scientists," unpublished paper delivered in Australia, 1994, available from author.

Chapter 5

1. Buchanan quoted in Susan Yoachum and David Tuller, "Right Makes Might in Iowa," *San Francisco Chronicle*, February 12, 1996: A1, 11.
2. Rauch (see bibliographic entry).
3. Bonnie Tinker, "Love Makes a Family," Presentation to 1995 United Nations International Women's Conference, Beijing, September 14.

Bibliography

· · · · · · · · · · ·

Abel, Emily. 1986. "Adult Daughters and Care for the Elderly," *Feminist Studies* 12, no. 3. Fall: 479–97.

Acker, Joan. 1973. "Women and Social Stratification: A Case of Intellectual Sexism," *American Journal of Sociology* 78, no. 4:936–945.

Ahrons, Constance R. *The Good Divorce*. New York: Harper-Collins, 1994.

Alexander, Shoshana. *In Praise of Single Parents: Mothers and Fathers Embracing the Challenge*. New York: Houghton Mifflin, 1994.

Allen, Katherine R. and David H. Demo, "The Families of Lesbians and Gay Men: A New Frontier in Family Research," *Journal of Marriage and the Family* 57 (February 1995): 111–27.

Andrews, Edmund L. "Panel Votes to Ban Online 'Indecency.' " *San Francisco Chronicle*. December 7, 1995, A1, 115.

Bane, Mary Jo. *Here to Stay: American Families in the Twentieth Century*. New York: Basic Books, 1976.

Batteiger, John. "Bigotry for Bucks." *San Francisco Bay Guardian*. April 7, 1993, 19.

Bauer, Gary L. 1993. "Family Values Matter!" *Focus on the Family Citizen* 7, n.5. May, 16.

Beck, Joan. "What's good for babies: Both parents," *The Press Democrat*. March 7, 1993, G1, G6.

Bell, Daniel. *The End of Ideology: On the Exhaustion of Political Ideas in the Fifties*. New York: Free Press, 1962.

Belkin, Lisa. "Bars to Equality of Sexes Seen as Eroding, Slowly." *New York Times*. August 20, 1989: A1, A16.

Benkov, Laura. *Reinventing the Family: Lesbian and Gay Parents.* New York: Crown, 1994.

Berger, Brigette and Peter Berger. *The War Over the Family.* New York: Anchor Press/Doubleday, 1983.

Berke, Richard L. "Two Top Republicans Soften Their Tone." *New York Times,* September 17, 1994a. A8.

———. "U.S. Voter Focus on Selves, Poll Says." *New York Times,* September 21, 1994b. A12.

Bernard, Jessie. *The Future of Marriage.* New York: World Publishing, 1972.

Blankenhorn, David. *Fatherless America: Confronting Our Most Urgent Social Problem.* New York: Basic Books, 1995.

Blankenhorn, David, Jean Bethke Elshtain and Steven Bayme, eds. *Rebuilding the Nest: A New Commitment to the American Family.* Milwaukee: Family Service America, 1990.

Blum, Linda. *Between Feminism and Labor: The Significance of the Comparable Worth Movement.* Berkeley and Los Angeles: University of California Press, 1991.

Blumstein, Philip and Pepper Schwartz. *American Couples.* New York: William Morrow, 1983.

Boh, Katja. "European Family Life Patterns—A Reappraisal," in Changing Patterns of European Family Life: A Comparative Analysis of 14 European Countries, Katja Boh, Maren Bak, et. al., eds., London: Routledge, 1989, 280.

Boswell, John. *Same-Sex Unions in Premodern Europe.* New York: Villard Books, 1994.

Bozett, Frederick W., ed. *Gay and Lesbian Parents.* New York: Praeger, 1987.

Brownstein, Ronald. 1994. "Democrats Find the Right's Stuff: Family Values." *Los Angeles Times,* August 1, 1994. A1, A23.

Bumpass, Larry and James Sweet. 1988. "Preliminary Evidence on Cohabitation," NSFH Working Paper No. 2, Center for Demography and Ecology, University of Wisconsin-Madison. September.

Bumpass, Larry and Teresa Castro. 1987. "Trends in Marital Disruption," Working Paper 87–20, Center for Demography and Ecology, University of Wisconsin-Madison, June.

Bureau of Labor Statistics. "Labor Force Participation Unchanged Among Mothers of Young Children." USDL 88-431. Washington: US Government Printing Office, 1988.

Burke, Phyllis. *Family Values: A Lesbian Mother's Fight for Her Son.* New York: Random House, 1993.

Caplow, Theodore, et. al. *Middletown Families: Fifty Years of Change and Continuity.* Toronto: Bantam Books, 1983.

Carlson, Allan. *The Swedish Experiment in Family Politics: The Myrdals and the Interwar Population Crisis.* New Brunswick: Transaction, 1990.

Charen, Mona. 1993. "Hey, Murphy, Quayle was right." *Orange County Register.* 29 March, B9.

Cheal, David. *Family and the State of Theory.* New York: Harvester Wheatsheaf, 1991.

Cherlin, Andrew J. *The Changing American Family and Public Policy.* Washington, DC: Urban Institute Press, 1988.

Chira, Susan. 1994. "Push to Revamp Ideal for American Fathers." *New York Times.* 19 June, 10.

———. Marriage, Divorce, Remarriage. Revised edition, 1992. Cambridge: Harvard University Press, 1981.

Chodorow, Nancy. *The Reproduction of Mothering.* Berkeley and Los Angeles: University of California Press, 1978.

Clifford, James. "Identity in Mashpee," in his *The Predicament of Culture,* Harvard University Press, 1988.

Clinton, Hillary Rodham. *It Takes A Village: And Other Lessons Children Teach Us.* New York: Simon & Schuster, 1996.

Coles, Robert and Jane Hallowell Cole. *Women of Crisis: Lives of Struggle and Hope.* New York: Delacorte Press/S. Lawrence, 1978.

The Compact Edition of the Oxford English Dictionary, Oxford University Press, 1971.

Connell, R. W. *Masculinities.* Berkeley and Los Angeles: University of California Press, 1995.

Coontz, Stephanie. *The Social Origins of Private Life: A History of American Families, 1600–1900.* London: Verso, 1988.

———. *The Way We Never Were: American Families and the Nostalgia Trap.* New York: Basic Books, 1992.

Council on Families in America. 1994. "Family and Child Well-Being: Eight Propositions." *Family Affairs* 6, n. 1–2. Winter, 11.

Dance, Betsy. 1996. "Is There a Father in the House?" *New Yorker,* January 8, 25.

Dao, James. 1995. "Ruling Lets Unwed Couples Adopt," *New York Times,* November 3, A11.

Davis, Kingsley. "Wives and Work: A Theory of the Sex-Role Revolution and its Consequences," in *Feminism, Children, and the New Families*, eds. Sanford Dornbusch and Myra Strober. New York: The Guilford Press, 1988.

Degler, Carl. *At Odds: Women and the Family in America from the Revolution to the Present*. Oxford and New York: Oxford University Press, 1980.

Demo, David H. 1992. "Parent-Child Relations: Assessing Recent Changes." *Journal of Marriage and the Family* 54 (February): 104.

Demo, David H. & Katharine R. Allen. 1996. "Diversity Within Lesbian and Gay Families: Challenges and Implications for Family Theory and Research." *Journal of Social and Personal Relationships*. 13, n.3

DeParle, Jason. 1993. "Census Reports a Sharp Increase Among Never-Married Mothers," *New York Times*, July 14, A1, 9.

DeParle, Jason. 1995. "Sheila Burke and the Attack Machine." *New York Times Magazine* 12 November, 35.

Derber, Charles. 1993. "Coming Glued: Communitarianism to the Rescue." *Tikkun* 8, n.4. (July/August): 27–30.

di Leonardo, Micaela. *The Varieties of Ethnic Experience: Kinship, Class, and Gender Among California Italian-Americans*. pp. 194–205. Ithaca: Cornell University Press, 1984.

Dilnot, Clive. 1986. "What is the Postmodern?" *Art History* 9, n.2. (June): 245–63.

Dinnerstein, Dorothy. *The Mermaid and the Minotaur: Sexual Arrangements and Human Malaise*. New York: Harper & Row, 1976.

Downey, Douglas B. & Brian Powell. 1993. "Do Children in Single-Parent Households Fare Better Living With Same-Sex Parents?" *Journal of Marriage and the Family*, 55 (February): 55–71.

Due, Linnea. *Joining The Tribe: Growing Up Gay and Lesbian in the 90's*. New York: Doubleday 1996.

Dunlap, David W. 1995. "Some States Trying to Stop Gay Marriages before They Start," *New York Times*, 15 March, A18.

Dunlap, David W. 1996. "Fearing a Toehold for Gay Marriage, Conservatives Rush to Bar the Door." *New York Times*, 6 March, A7.

Ehrenreich, Barbara. "Two, Three, Many Husbands." In *The Worst Years of Our Lives: Irreverant Notes From A Decade of Greed*. 183–87. New York: Pantheon, 1990.

Ehrenreich, Barbara. *Fear of Falling: The Inner Life of the Middle Class*. New York: Pantheon, 1989.

Ehrensaft, Diane. *Parenting Together: Men and Women Sharing the Care of Their Children.* New York: Free Press, 1987.

Epstein, Barbara. *The Politics of Domesticity: Women, Evangelism and Temperance in Nineteenth-Century America.* New York: Wesleyan University Press, 1977.

Eskridge, Jr, William N. 1993. "A History of Same-Sex Marriage." *Virginia Law Review.* 79:1419–1513.

Evans, Sara. *Born for Liberty: A History of Women in America.* New York: Free Press, 1989.

Fairbank, Maslin, Maullins Associates. "National Health and Safety Study: Summary of Results." Santa Monica and San Francisco, CA: October 1995.

Ferguson, James. "Migration, Mineworkers, and 'the Modern Family' on the Zambian Copperbelt." Paper presented at American Anthropological Association Meetings, San Francisco, December 1992.

Fields, Suzanne. 1993. "Murphy's Chorus of Enlightened Celebrities." *Orange County Register.* March 29, B9.

Fiske, John. *Media Matters: Everyday Culture and Political Change.* Minneapolis: University of Minnesota Press, 1994.

Flaks, David K. 1994. "Gay and Lesbian Families: Judicial Assumptions, Scientific Realities." *William and Mary Bill of Rights Journal* 3, n.1. Summer:345–72.

Flammang, Janet. 1985. "Female Officials in the Feminist Capital: The Case of Santa Clara County," *Western Political Quarterly* 38, no.1. (March): 94–118.

———. "Women Made a Difference: Comparable Worth in San Jose," in *The Women's Movements of the United States and Western Europe,* eds. Ira Katznelson and Carole Mueller. pp. 290–309. Philadelphia: Temple University Press, 1987.

"The Forgotten Half: Pathways to Success for America's Youth and Young Families." Washington, DC: William T. Grant Foundation Commission on Work, Family and Citizenship, November, 1988.

Francis, David R. 1990. "Study Finds Steep Inequality in Wealth," *San Francisco Chronicle* March 30, A19.

Frazier, E. Franklin. *The Negro Family in the United States.* Chicago: University of Chicago Press, 1939.

Friedan, Betty. *The Feminine Mystique.* New York: Norton, 1963.

———. *The Second Stage.* New York: Summit Books, 1981.

Furstenberg, Jr., Frank. "Good Dads, Bad Dads." In *The Changing Amer-*

ican Family and Public Policy. Andrew Cherlin, ed. Washington, D.C.: Urban Institute Press, 1988.

Furstenberg, Jr., Frank and Andrew J. Cherlin. *Divided Families: What Happens to Children When Parents Part.* Cambridge: Harvard University Press, 1991.

Gerson, Kathleen. *Hard Choices: How Women Decide About Work, Career, and Motherhood.* Berkeley and Los Angeles: University of California Press, 1985.

——. *No Man's Land: Men's Changing Commitments to Family and Work.* New York: Basic Books, 1993.

Gibbs, Nancy. "The War Against Feminism," *Time,* March 9, 1998, 55.

Giddings, Paula. *When and Where I Enter: The Impact of Black Women on Race and Sex in America.* New York: William Morrow, 1984.

Gil de Lamadrid, Maria. 1993. "Expanding the Definition of Family: A Universal Issue." *Berkeley Women's Law Journal.* 8:170–79.

Gilder, George. *Men and Marriage.* Gretna, LA: Pelican Publishing Co., 1986.

Gilligan, Carol. *In a Different Voice: Psychological Development and Woman's Psychology.* Cambridge, MA: Harvard University Press, 1982.

Gillis, John. *A World of Their Own Making: Myth, Ritual, and the Quest for Family Values.* New York: Basic Books, 1996.

——. "What's Beyond the Debate on Family Values?" Paper delivered at the annual meetings of the American Sociological Association. Los Angeles, August 6, 1994.

Glenn, Norval D. "The Re-evaluation of Family Change by American Social Scientists." Paper presented to Committee for the International Year of the Family of the Catholic Archdiocese of Melbourne, 1994.

Glenn, Norval D. 1994. "A Plea for Objective Assessment of the Notion of Family Decline." *Journal of Marriage and the Family* 55, n.3 (August): 543.

Goldberg, Carey. 1996. "Virtual Marriages for Same-Sex Couples." *New York Times,* 26 March, A8.

Goode, William J. *World Revolution and Family Patterns.* New York: Free Press, 1963.

Gordon, Linda. *Heroes of Their Own Lives.* New York: Viking, 1988.

——. *Pitied But Not Entitled: Single Mothers and the History of Welfare.* New York: Free Press, 1994.

Gordon, Tuula. 1994. "Single Women and Familism: Challenge from the Margins." *European Journal of Women's Studies.* 1(2):165–82.

Greenberg Research. 1994. Poll Sponsored by Democratic Leadership Council. November 8–9. Roper Center Public Opinion Online database.

Gregory, Steven. "Time To Make The Doughnuts: On the Politics of Subjugation in the Inner City." Paper presented at American Anthropological Association Meetings, Washington, D.C., November 1993.

Griscom, Joan. "The Case of Sharon Kowalski and Karen Thompson." in P. S. Rothenberg, ed., *Race, Class, and Gender in the United States: An Integrated Study*. New York: St. Martin's Press, 1992.

Griswold, Robert. *Fatherhood in America*. New York: Basic Books, 1993.

Grossberg, Michael. 1983. "Who Gets the Child? Custody, Guardianship, and The Rise of A Judicial Patriarchy in Nineteenth-Century America," *Feminist Studies* 9, n.2 (Summer): 235–60.

Gutis, Philip J. 1989. "What Makes a Family? Traditional Limits Are Challenged." *New York Times*, 31 August, B1.

Gutman, Herbert G. 1975. "Persistent Myths about the Afro-American Family." *Journal of Interdisciplinary History* VI, no. 2. 1 (Autumn): 184.

Halle, David. *America's Working Man*. Chicago: University of Chicago Press, 1984.

Hartmann, Heidi. "Capitalism, Patriarchy, and Job Segregation by Sex," in *Capitalist Patriarchy and the Case for Socialist-Feminism*, ed., Zillah Eisenstein. New York: Monthly Review Press, 1979.

Harrison, Bennett and Barry Bluestone. *The Great U-Turn*. New York: Basic Books, 1988.

Heller, Scott. 1995. "Finding a Common Purpose." *Chronicle of Higher Education*, March 31, A10, A16.

Henry, Vickie L. 1993. "A Tale of Three Women: A Survey of the Rights and Responsibilities of Unmarried Women Who Conceive by Alternative Insemination and a Model for Legislative Reform," *American Journal of Law & Medicine* XIX, n.3:297.

Herscher, Elaine. 1995. "After Reconsidering, Montana Junks Gay Sex Bill," *San Francisco Chronicle*, March 24.

Hewlet, Sylvia Ann. *A Lesser Life: The Myth of Women's Liberation in America*. New York: William Morrow, 1986.

Hochschild, Arlie. "Inside the Clockwork of Male Careers." In *Women and the Power to Change*. Florence Howe, ed. New York: McGraw-Hill, 1975.

Hochschild, Arlie with Anne Machung. *The Second Shift: Working Parents and the Revolution at Home*. New York: Viking Penguin, 1989.

Holland, Jean. *The Silicon Syndrome: A Survival Handbook for Couples.* Palo Alto, CA: Coastlight Press, 1988.

Humphries, Jane. 1977. "The Working-Class Family, Women's Liberation and Class Struggle: The Case of Nineteenth-Century British History," *Review of Radical Political Economics* 9 (Fall): 25–41.

Hunter, Nan D. 1991. "Marriage, Law, and Gender: A Feminist Inquiry." *Law & Sexuality*, 1, n.1:9–30.

Joffe, Carole. *Doctors of Conscience.* Boston: Beacon Press, 1996.

Johnson, Colleen Leashy. *Ex-Familia: Grandparents, Parents and Children Adjust to Divorce.* New Brunswick: Rutgers University Press, 1988.

Johnson, Dirk. 1991. "No-Fault Divorce Is Under Attack," *New York Times*, 12 February, A8.

Jones, Jacqueline. *Labor of Love, Labor of Sorrow: Black Women, Work and The Family, From Slavery to the Present.* New York: Basic Books, 1985.

Kamarck, Elaine Ciulla and William A. Galston, "Putting Children First: A Progressive Family Policy for the 1990s," Progressive Policy Institute pamphlet, September 27, 1990.

Kandiyoti, Deniz. 1988. "Bargaining With Patriarchy," *Gender & Society* 2, n.3. (September): 274–90.

Kershner, Vlae. 1989. "The Payoff for Educated Workers," *San Francisco Chronicle*, 26 December, A2.

Kessler-Harris, Alice and Karen Sacks. "The Demise of Domesticity," in *Women, Households and the Economy*, ed. Lourdes Beneria and Catharine R. Stimpson. New Brunswick, NJ: Rutgers University Press, 1987.

Kinzer, Stephen. 1994. "$650 a Baby: Germany to Pay to Stem Decline in Births," *New York Times*, 25 November, A1.

Klein, Joe. "The Out-of-Wedlock Question." *Newsweek.* December 13, 1993.

Koedt, Anne. "The Myth of the Vaginal Orgasm." in *Liberation Now! Writings From the Women's Liberation Movement.* New York: Dell, 1970.

Komarovsky, Mirra, with Jane H. Philips. *Blue-Collar Marriage.* New York: Summit Books, 1986.

Kranish, Michael. 1993. "In Bully Pulpit, Preaching Values." *Boston Globe*, 10 Dec, 17.

Kuhn, Sara and Barry Bluestone. "Economic Restructuring and Female Labor: The Impact of Industrial Change on Women," in Beneria and Stimpson, eds., *Women, Households and the Economy.* New Brunswick: Rutgers University Press, 1987.

Kurdek, Lawrence. 1993. "The Allocation of Household Labor in Gay,

Lesbian, and Heterosexual Married Couples," *Journal of Social Issues* 49, n.3:127–39.

Kurdek, L. A. & J. P. Schmitt. 1985. "Relationship Quality of Gay Men in Closed or Open Relationships," *Journal of Homosexuality* 12, n.2:85–99.

Laird, Joan. 1993. "Lesbian and Gay Families." in Froma Walsh, ed. *Normal Family Processes*, Second edition. New York: Guilford Press, 1993.

Lamphere, Louise, Felipe Gonzales, Patricia Zavella and Peter Evans. *Sunbelt Working Mothers: Reconciling Family and Factory*. Ithaca: Cornell University Press, 1993.

Lasch, Christopher. 1991. "Misreading The Facts About Families." *Commonweal*, 22 Feb, 136.

Laslett, Peter. *The World We Have Lost: England Before the Industrial Age*. New York: Charles Scribner's Sons, 1965.

Lefkowitz, Jay. 1993. "Where Dad Belongs." *Wall Street Journal*, 18 June, A12.

Leo, John. "Promoting No-Dad Families," *U.S. News & World Report* 118, n.19 May 15, 1995, 26.

Levitan, Sar A. et. al. *What's Happening to American Families? Tensions, Hopes, Realities*. Revised edition. Baltimore: Johns Hopkins University Press, 1988.

Liebow, Elliot. *Tally's Corner*. Boston: Little, Brown and Co., 1967.

Lipset, Seymour Martin. *Political Man*. Garden City, NY: Doubleday, 1963.

Lynch, F. R. "Nonghetto Gays: An Ethnography of Suburban Homosexuals." In Gilbert Herdt, ed., *Gay Culture in America: Essays From the Field* (Boston: Beacon Press, 1992):165–201.

Mainardi, Pat. "The Politics of Housework," in *Sisterhood is Powerful: An Anthology of Writings from the Women's Liberation Movement*, ed. Robin Morgan. New York: Vintage, 1970.

Malone, Michael S. "Family in Crisis," *Santa Clara Magazine*, Spring, 1989.

Marcus, George, ed. *New Locations*. Santa Fe: School of American Research Press, 1997 (in press).

———. 1993. Power/Knowledge Shifts in America's Present Fin-De-Siècle: A Proposal for a School of American Research Advanced Seminar.

May, Elaine. *Homeward Bound: American Families in the Cold War Era*. New York: Basic Books, 1988.

May, Martha. "Bread Before Roses: American Workingmen, Labor Unions and The Family Wage," in *Women, Work & Protest: A Century of U.S.*

Women's Labor History, ed, Ruth Milkman. Boston: Routledge & Kegan Paul, 1985.

McLanahan, Sara and Larry L. Bumpass. 1988. "Intergenerational Consequences of Family Disruption." *American Journal of Sociology* 94: 130–52.

McLanahan, Sara. 1994. "The Consequences of Single Motherhood." *The American Prospect.* n. 18.

McLanahan, Sara and Karen Booth. 1989. "Mother-Only Families: Problems, Prospects, and Politics." *Journal of Marriage and the Family* 51. August: 557–80.

McLaughlin, Steven D. et al. *The Changing Lives of American Women.* Chapel Hill: University of North Carolina Press, 1988.

Messer-Davidow, Ellen. 1993. "Manufacturing the Attack on Liberalized Higher Education." *Social Text* 36:40–80.

Millar, Jane. 1994. "State, Family and Personal Responsibility: The Changing Balance for Lone Mothers in the United Kingdom." *Feminist Review* 48:24–39.

Miller, Neil. *Out in the World: Gay and Lesbian Life from Buenos Aires to Bangkok.* New York: Random House, 1992.

Minter, Shannon. "U.S.A." in Rachel Rosenbloom, ed. *Unspoken Rules: Sexual Orientation and Women's Human Rights.* San Francisco: International Gay and Lesbian Human Rights Commission, 1995.

Mintz, Steven and Susan Kellogg. *Domestic Revolutions: A Social History of American Family Life.* New York: Free Press, 1988.

Mohr, Richard. *A More Perfect Union. Why Straight America Must Stand Up for Gay Rights.* Boston: Beacon, 1994.

Moore, Kristin. "Report to Congress on Out-Of-Wedlock Childbearing." Washington D.C.: Child Trends, Inc., 1994.

Moore, Teresa. "Fear of Violence Rising Among 1990s Youth," *San Francisco Chronicle*, December 7, 1995, A1, A15.

"Most Regard Family Highly," 1989. *New York Times*, 10 October, A18.

Moynihan, Daniel Patrick. *The Negro Family: The Case for National Action.* Washington, D.C.: U.S. Department of Labor, 1965.

———. 1996. "Congress Builds a Coffin," *New York Review of Books* XLIII, n.1, 11 January 33–36.

———. 1993. "Defining Deviancy Down." *American Scholar* (Winter): 17–30.

Murray, Charles. 1993. "The Time Has Come to Put a Stigma Back on Illegitimacy." *Wall Street Journal* 29 October, Forum.

————. 1993. "The Emerging White Underclass and How to Save It." *Philadelphia Inquirer* 15 November, A15.

National Center for Lesbian Rights. "Our Day in Court—Against Each Other: Intra-Community Disputes Threaten All of Our Rights." In Rubenstein, ed. *Lesbians, Gay Men and the Law*, 1993.

National Commission on Children. *Beyond Rhetoric: A New American Agenda for Children and Families.* Washington, D.C.: Library of Congress, 1991.

National Research Council. *Summary Report 1990: Doctorate Recipients from United States Universities.* Washington, D.C.: National Academy Press, 1991.

National Science Foundation. *Science and Engineering Degrees: 1966–1989, A Source Book.* NSF 91-314. Washington, D.C.: National Science Foundation, 1991.

Newman, Katharine S. *Declining Fortunes: The Withering of the American Dream.* New York: Basic Books, 1993.

————. *Falling From Grace: The Experience of Downward Mobility in the American Middle Class.* New York: The Free Press, 1988.

Newton, Judith. 1995. "A Feminist Among Promise Keepers," *Davis Enterprise*, 8 October, A6.

Newton, Judith and Judith Stacey. 1992–93. "Learning Not to Curse, or Feminist Predicaments in Cultural Criticism By Men: Our Movie Date with Stephen Greenblatt and James Clifford." *Cultural Critique* 23: 51–81.

————. "Ms. Representations: Feminist Dilemmas in Studying Academic Men." *In Women Writing Culture/Culture Writing Women.* ed. Ruth Behar and Deborah Gordon. Berkeley: University of California Press, 1995.

————. "The Men We Left Behind Us," in *Sociology and Cultural Studies.* ed. Elizabeth Long. New York: Basil Blackwell, forthcoming.

Oakley, Ann. *The Sociology of Housework.* New York: Pantheon, 1974.

Ortner, Sherry. "The Virgin and the State," *Feminist Studies* 4, no.3 (October): 19–35.

Parsons, Talcott and Robert Bales. *Family, Socialization and Interaction Process.* Glencoe, IL: Free Press, 1955.

Patterson, Charlotte J. 1992. "Children of Lesbian and Gay Parents." *Child Development* 63:1025–42.

Peplau, Letitia. "Research on Homosexual Couples: An Overview." *In Gay Relationships.* John P. De Cecco, ed. New York: Haworth Press, 1988.

———. "Lesbian and Gay Relationships." In *Homosexuality: Research Implications for Public Policy*. John C. Gonsiorek and James D. Weinrich, eds. Newbury Park: Sage, 1991.

Polikoff, Nancy. "Gender and Child-Custody Determinations: Exploding the Myths," in *Families, Politics, and Public Policy: A Feminist Dialogue on Women and the State*, ed. Irene Diamond, New York: Longman, 1983.

———. 1990. "This Child Does Have Two Mothers: Redefining Parenthood to Meet the Needs of Children in Lesbian-Mother and Other Nontraditional Families," *Georgetown Law Journal*, vol. 78.

———. 1993 "We Will Get What We Ask For: Why Legalizing Gay and Lesbian Marriage Will Not 'Dismantle the Legal Structure of Gender in Every Marriage'," *Virginia Law Review*, vol. 79: 1549–50.

Popenoe, David. *Disturbing the Nest: Family Change and Decline in Modern Societies*. New York: Aldine de Gruyter, 1988.

———. 1992. "The Controversial Truth: The Two-Parent Family is Better." *New York Times*, 26 December, 13.

———. 1992. "Modern Marriage: Revising the Cultural Script." Council on Families in America Working Paper, no. WP17 New York: Institute for American Values. August 2.

———. 1993a. "American Family Decline, 1960–1990: A Review and Appraisal." *Journal of Marriage and the Family* 55(3):527–44.

———. 1993b. "Scholars Should Worry About the Disintegration of the American Family." *Chronicle of Higher Education* 14 (April): A48.

———. 1994. "What's Behind the Family Values Debate?" Paper presented at the annual meetings of the American Sociological Association. Los Angeles, August 7, 1994.

———. 1994. The Family Condition of America: Cultural Change and Public Policy. Pp. 81–112 in *Values and Public Policy*. Henry J. Aaron, Thomas E. Mann & Timothy Taylor, eds. Washington, D.C.: The Brookings Institute, 98.

Probyn, Elsbeth. "Television's Unheimlich Home," in *The Politics of Everyday Fear*, Brian Massumi, ed. Minneapolis: University of Minnesota Press, 1994.

Raskin, Louise, ed. *Different Mothers: Sons and Daughters of Lesbians Talk About Their Lives*. Pittsburgh: Cleis Press, 1990.

Rauch, Jonathan. 1994. "A Pro-Gay, Pro-Family Policy," *Wall Street Journal*, 29 November, A22.

Reinhold, Susan. 1994. "Through The Parliamentary Looking Glass: 'Real' and 'Pretend' Families in Contemporary British Politics," *Feminist Review* n.48, (Autumn): 61–78.

Remafedi, Gary. ed. *Death by Denial*. Boston: Alyson Publications, 1994.

Rich, Adrienne. 1980. "Compulsory Heterosexuality and Lesbian Existence." *Signs*. 5, n.2. (Summer).

Rivera, Rhonda R. "Legal Issues in Gay and Lesbian Parenting," in *Gay and Lesbian Parents*, Frederick W. Bozett, ed. New York: Praeger, 1987.

Rose, Stephen and David Fasenfest. "Family Incomes in the 1980s: New Pressure on Wives, Husbands and Young Adults." *Working Paper* No. 103, Washington, D.C.: Economic Policy Institute, November 1988.

Rosenbloom, Rachel, ed. "Unspoken Rules: Sexual Orientation and Women's Human Rights." San Francisco: International Gay and Lesbian Human Rights Commission, 1995

Rosenfelt, Deborah and Judith Stacey. 1987. "Second Thoughts on the Second Wave." *Feminist Studies* 13(2):341–61.

Rubin, Gayle. "The Traffic in Women: Notes on the 'Political Economy' of Sex." In *Toward an Anthropology of Women*, ed. Rayna Reiter. New York: Monthly Review, 1975.

Rubin, Lillian. *Worlds of Pain: Life in the Working Class Family*. New York: Basic Books, 1976.

———. *Families on the Faultline: America's Working Class Speaks About The Family, The Economy, Race, and Ethnicity*. New York: HarperCollins, 1994.

Rubenstein, William B. ed. *Lesbians, Gay Men, and the Law*. New York: New Press, 1993.

Ruddick, Sarah. *Maternal Thinking: Toward a Politics of Peace*. Boston: Beacon Press, 1989.

Ryan, Alan. "No Easy Way Out," *New Yorker*. September 11, 1995, p. 90.

Ryan, Mary. 1982. "The Empire of the Mother: American Writing about Domesticity 1830–1860," *Women & History* n.2/3 (Summer/Fall).

Sandalow, Marc and David Tuller. 1995. "White House Tells Gays It Backs Them," *San Francisco Chronicle*, 21 October, A2.

Sandqvist, Karin and Bengt-Erik Andersson. 1992. "Thriving Families in the Swedish Welfare State." *Public Interest* n.109:114–17.

Schnaiberg, Allan and Sheldon Goldenberg. 1989. "From Empty Nest to Crowded Nest: The Dynamics of Incompletely-Launched Young Adults," *Social Problems* 36, no.3 (June): 251–69.

Schneider, David M. and Raymond T. Smith. *Class Differences and Sex Roles in American Kinship and Family Structure.* Englewood Cliffs, NJ: Prentice-Hall, 1973.

Schulenberg, John. *Gay Parenting.* New York: Doubleday, 1985.

Schwartz, Pepper. 1995. "Children's New Bonds: Para-Dads, Para-Moms." *New York Times,* 9 November, B1, B4.

Sedgwick, Eve. "How to Bring Your Kids Up Gay," In *Fear of a Queer Planet: Queer Politics and Social Theory,* Michael Warner, ed. Minneapolis: University of Minnesota Press, 1993.

Segal, Lynne. *Slow Motion: Changing Masculinities, Changing Men.* London, Virago, 1990.

Seligman, Jean. "Variations on a Theme." *Newsweek* (special edition), Winter/Spring, 1990, 38.

Seligson, Susan. "Seeds of Doubt," *Atlantic Monthly,* (March 1995), 28.

Sennet, Richard. 1994. "The New Censorship." *Contemporary Sociology* 23(4):487–91.

Shellenbanger, Sue. 1995. "Bill Galston Tells The President: My Son Needs Me More." *Wall Street Journal,* 21 June, B1.

Sherman, Suzanne, ed. *Lesbian and Gay Marriage: Private Commitments, Public Ceremonies.* Philadelphia: Temple University Press, 1992.

Shogren, Elizabeth. 1995. "Republicans Get Lesson in Family Values." *San Francisco Sunday Examiner and Chronicle,* 17 December, C10.

Shogren, Elizabeth. 1994. "Traditional Family Nearly the Exception, Census Finds." *Los Angeles Times,* 30 August 30, A1, A28.

Shorter, Edward. *The Making of the Modern Family.* New York: Basic Books, 1975.

———. 1995. "Yearning for the Family of Yore." *Readings: A Journal of Reviews and Commentary in Mental Health,* (September): 14.

Skolnick, Arlene. *Embattled Paradise: The American Family in An Age of Uncertainty.* New York: Basic Books, 1994.

Smeeding, Timothy M. "Why the U.S. Antipoverty System Doesn't Work Very Well," *Challenge,* January-February 1992, 33.

Smith, Joan. "Marginalized Labor Forces During the Reagan Recovery." Paper presented to Society for the Study of Social Problems, Berkeley, California, August 19, 1989.

Smothers, Ronald. 1993. "Tell It to Mom, Dad, and the Authorities." *New York Times,* Week in Review, 14 November, 2.

Spigel, Lynn. *Make Room for TV: Television and the Family Ideal in Postwar America.* Chicago: University of Chicago Press, 1992.

————. 1995. "From the Dark Ages to the Golden Era: Women's Memories and Television Reruns." *Screen.* 36(1):14–31.

Stacey, Judith. 1983. "The New Conservative Feminism." *Feminist Studies* 9(3):559–83.

————. *Patriarchy and Socialist Revolution in China.* Berkeley: University of California Press, 1983.

————. "Are Feminists Afraid to Leave Home? The Challenge of Profamily Feminism." In *What is Feminism?* Juliet Mitchell and Ann Oakley, ed. London: Basil Blackwell, 1986.

————. *Brave New Families: Stories of Domestic Upheaval in Late Twentieth Century America.* New York: Basic Books, 1990.

————. "The New Family Values Crusaders." *The Nation,* July 25–August 1, 1994, 22.

Stacey, Judith, and Susan Elizabeth Gerard. "We are not Doormats: The Influence of Feminism on Contemporary Evangelicalism in the United States," in *Negotiating Gender in American Culture,* eds. Faye Ginsburg and Anna Tsing. Boston: Beacon Press, 1990.

Stack, Carol. *All Our Kin: Strategies for Survival in a Black Community.* New York: Harper and Row, 1974.

Strand, Douglas Alan and Kenneth Sherrill. 1993. "Electoral Bugaboos? The Impact of Attitudes Toward Gay Rights and Feminism on the 1992 Presidential Vote." Paper delivered at the annual meetings of the American Political Science Association, Washington D.C.

Strober, Myra. "Two-Earner Families," in Sanford M. Dornbusch & Myra H. Strober, eds, *Feminism, Children, and the New Families.* New York: The Guilford Press, 1988.

Suggs, Donald and Mandy Carter. 1993. "Cincinnati's Odd Couple." *New York Times,* 13 December, A11.

Sullivan, Andrew. "Here Comes the Groom: A (Conservative) Case for Gay Marriage." *New Republic.* v 201, n.9. August 28, 1989, 20–21.

Tasker, Fiona & Susan Golombok. 1995. "Adults Raised as Children in Lesbian Families," *American Journal of Orthopsychiatry* 65, n.2, (April): 203–215.

Taylor, Ella. *Primetime Families: Television Culture in Postwar America.* Berkeley: University of California Press, 1989.

Toner, Robin. 1993. "Republican Factions Gather Under One Tent, Then Argue." *New York Times,* 11 May.

Traube, Elizabeth. 1995. "Family Matters." *Visual Anthropology* 9, n.1 56–73.

United Nations Committee on the Family. 1994. "Guiding Principles On The Family." Vienna, United Nations Vienna International Centre.

United Nations Committee on the Family. 1994. "Family in Crisis." Vienna, United Nations International Centre.

United Nations. *The World's Women 1970–1990: Trends and Statistics*, New York, 1991.

U.S. Bureau of the Census. Census of Population for 1960, 1970 and 1980.

———. Statistical Abstract of the United States, 1981.

Van Horn, Susan Householder. *Women, Work and Fertility, 1900–1986*. New York: New York University Press, 1988.

Vobejda, Barbara. 1992. "Family Gap Found in Post-Election Poll." *San Francisco Chronicle*, 27 November, A4.

Walker, Henry A. "Black-White Differences in Marriage and Family Patterns," in Sanford M. Dornbusch and Myra H. Strober, eds. *Feminism, Children, and the New Families*. New York: Guilford Press, 1988.

Wallerstein, Judith and Joan B. Kelly. *Surviving the Breakup: How Children and Parents Cope with Divorce*. New York: Basic Books, 1980.

Wallerstein, Judith S. and Sandra Blakeslee. *Second Chances: Men, Women, and Children A Decade After Divorce*. New York: Ticknor & Fields, 1989.

Wallis, Claudia. "Onward, Women!" *Time*, December 4, 1989, 80–89.

Walshock, Mary Lindenstein. "Occupational Values and Family Roles," in *Working Women and Families*, ed., Karen Wolk Feinstein. Beverly Hills: Sage Publications, 1979.

Weber, Max. "The Sociology of Charismatic Authority." In *From Max Weber: Essays in Sociology*. Hans Gerth and C. Wright Mills, ed. 1958 edition, New York: Oxford University Press, 1946.

Weitzman, Lenore J. *The Divorce Revolution: The Unexpected Social and Economic Consequences for Women and Children in America*. New York: Free Press, 1985.

Welter, Barbara. 1996. "The Cult of True Womanhood, 1820–1860," *American Quarterly* 18: 151–74.

Wennemo, Irene. *Sharing the Costs of Children*. Stockholm: Swedish Institute for Social Research, 1994.

Weston, Kath. *Families We Choose: Lesbians, Gays, Kinship*. New York: Columbia University Press, 1991.

White, Deborah Gray. *Ar'n't I a Woman? Female Slaves in the Plantation South*. New York: Norton, 1985.

White, Evelyn C. 1994. "Christian Right Tries to Capitalize on Anti-Gay Views." *San Francisco Chronicle*, 12 January, A6.

Whitehead, Barbara Dafoe. 1993. "Dan Quayle Was Right." *The Atlantic* 271, no.4. (April): 47–84.

———. 1992. "A New Familism?" *Family Affairs* 5, no.1–2 (Summer): 5.

———. 1994. "Was Dan Quayle Right?" *Family Affairs* 6, n.1–2. (Winter): 13.

Wikler, Daniel and Norma J. Wikler. 1991. "Turkey-baster Babies: The Demedicalization of Artificial Insemination." *Milbank Quarterly.* 69, n. 1:5–40.

Williams, Patricia J. "Different Drummer Please, Marchers!" *The Nation*, October 30, 1995, 493.

Williams, Walter L. *The Spirit and the Flesh: Sexual Diversity in American Indian Culture.* Boston: Beacon Press, 1986.

Wilson, James Q. 1993. "The Family-Values Debate." *Commentary* 95(4): 24–31.

Wilson, William J. *The Truly Disadvantaged: The Inner City, The Underclass, and Public Policy.* Chicago: University of Chicago Press, 1987.

Winkler, Karen. "Communitarians Move Their Ideas Outside Academic Arena." *Chronicle of Higher Education*, April 21, 1993, A7.

Wilensky, Harold. 1990. "Common Problems, Divergent Policies: An 18-Nation Study of Family Policy," *Public Affairs Reporter*, 31, n.3 (May): 1–3.

Willis, Doug. 1996. "Wilson to Unveil Welfare and Pro-Family Reforms." *Sacramento Bee*, 8 January, A1, A2.

Wolfe, Alan. *Whose Keeper? Social Science and Moral Obligation.* Berkeley: University of California Press, 1989.

Wolfson, Evan. "Crossing the Threshold: Equal Marriage Rights For Lesbians and Gay Men and the Intra-Community Critique," *Review of Law & Social Change*, XXI, n.3 (1994–95).

"Working Wives Keep America's Families Out of Red," 1994. *San Francisco Chronicle*, 14 March, A5.

Wright, Eric Olin, Cynthia Costello, David Hacker and Joey Sprague. 1982. "The American Class Structure," *American Sociological Review* 47 no. 6:709–26.

——— and Bill Martin. 1987. "The Transformation of the American Class Structure, 1960–1980," *American Journal of Sociology* 93, no.1: 1–29.

Yellowbird, Michael and C. Matthew Snipp. "American Indian Families," in Ronald Taylor, ed., *Minority Families in the United States: A Multicultural Perspective.* Englewood Cliffs, NJ, Prentice Hall, 1994.

Yoachum, Susan. 1994. "Small Minority Voter Turnout a Product of Apathy and Anger." *San Francisco Chronicle*, 22 September, A4.

Young, Michael and Peter Willmott. *Family and Kinship in East London.* Middlesex, England: Penguin, 1962.

Zavella, Patricia. "Sunbelt Hispanics on the Line." Paper presented at History and Theory Conference, University of California, Irvine, April, 1989.

Index

Library of Congress Cataloging-in-Publication Data

Stacey, Judith.
    In the name of the family : rethinking family values in a
postmodern age / Judith Stacey
        p.   cm.
    Includes bibliographical references and index.
    ISBN 0-8070-0432-4 (cloth)
    ISBN 0-8070-0433-2 (paper)
    1. Family—United States. 2. Social values—United States.
3. Social values—Political aspects—United States. 4. United
States—Social conditions—1980–   I. Title.
HQ536.S718   1996
306.85´0973—dc20

                                            96-7988

University
of Windsor

Date Due